THE EDUCATION WARS

Also by Jennifer C. Berkshire

A Wolf at the Schoolhouse Door
(co-authored with Jack Schneider)

Also by Jack Schneider

A Wolf at the Schoolhouse Door
(co-authored with Jennifer Berkshire)

Off the Mark

Beyond Test Scores

Excellence for All

From the Ivory Tower to the Schoolhouse

To Melissa —
Thanks for all you
do for kids!

THE EDUCATION WARS

A CITIZEN'S GUIDE AND DEFENSE MANUAL

Jennifer C. Berkshire
and Jack Schneider

THE
NEW
PRESS

NEW YORK
LONDON

Requests for permission to reproduce selections from this book should be made
through our website: https://thenewpress.com/contact.

Published in the United States by The New Press, New York, 2024
Distributed by Two Rivers Distribution

ISBN 978-1-62097-854-2 (hc)
ISBN 978-1-62097-871-9 (ebook)
CIP data is available

The New Press publishes books that promote and enrich public discussion and
understanding of the issues vital to our democracy and to a more equitable world.
These books are made possible by the enthusiasm of our readers; the support of a
committed group of donors, large and small; the collaboration of our many partners
in the independent media and the not-for-profit sector; booksellers, who often hand-
sell New Press books; librarians; and above all by our authors.

www.thenewpress.com

Book design and composition by Bookbright Media
This book was set in Sabon and Trade Gothic

Printed in the United States of America

10 9 8 7 6 5 4 3 2 1

Contents

THE EDUCATION WARS

Introduction

In the summer of 2023, Roy Cooper, the Democratic governor of North Carolina, declared a state of emergency. The occasion was not an impending hurricane or a river that had overflowed its banks; instead, it was a series of bills advancing through the Republican-controlled legislature—bills taking aim at the Tar Heel State's public schools. "It's clear that the Republican legislature is aiming to choke the life out of public education," said Cooper. If passed, he warned, the new laws would "set back our schools for a generation."[1]

Cooper singled out a sweeping expansion of North Carolina's private school voucher program for particular criticism. The GOP plan, he warned, would pour billions of dollars from the state's taxpayers into private schools that could pick and choose their students with no accountability to the public. And while even the wealthiest residents of the state could now get their children's private school tuition paid for by taxpayers, the real cost would be borne by students in the public schools, especially those in poor and rural parts of North Carolina, whose schools would face steep cuts.

In North Carolina, the school culture wars have provided the backdrop to a growing push to privatize public education. State legislators, backed by groups like Moms for Liberty, cite an ever-changing list of outrages—including Covid-mitigation efforts, critical race theory, and "gender ideology"—as they make the case for putting parents in charge and "funding students, not systems." While they use the familiar rhetoric about failing schools and inadequate test scores, the private schools they hold up as exemplary aren't part of North Carolina's accountability system at all—student performance simply isn't tracked by the state. Nor do they require licensed teachers. Indeed, one of the religious schools that taxpayers now pay for students to attend doesn't even require that its teachers have college degrees, just that they demonstrate the ability to speak in tongues.

North Carolina isn't alone. Across the United States, the flames of culture war are tearing through communities. But public education advocates see these conflagrations for what they are: distractions. The real policy goal, which is as divisive as it is unpopular, is to dismantle public schools as we know them. In the words of James E. Ford, executive director of the Center for Racial Equity in Education: "It's about robbing young families and communities of access to upward mobility through the destabilizing of traditional public schools."[2]

School Wars

Every few generations, the forces of chance and opportunism carry the nation's political and cultural conflicts into the schools. And suddenly Americans wake up to the fragility of the peace. We realize, once again, just how much there is to fight about.

As we write this book, millions of Americans are well past being concerned. Alarmed by a wave of reactionary policies in red states—limiting what teachers can teach and students can learn—parents, teachers, and students have taken to the ramparts. Conservatives, meanwhile, describe a dystopia in which public schools have been captured by the left, calling for them to be purged or abandoned in favor of schools that are explicitly Christian and patriotic. Any sense of the common interests that taxpayer-funded education depends upon has dissolved beneath our feet.

As readers of history will know, we've been here before. For as long as there have been public schools, there have been battles over what they should look like. As states enacted laws requiring young people to attend school in the nineteenth century, some parents revolted, declaring that they didn't co-parent with the government. Within a few decades, we were fighting over the role of religion in school, and whether teaching evolution was tantamount to leading kids away from the church. Twice during the twentieth century, panics over Communist infiltration led to reckless campaigns against educators and battles over the curriculum. And nearly as soon as the second Red Scare abated, we began to fight over sex education, the expansion of LGBTQ rights in schools, and "secular humanism"—yet another panic over the fear that schools were steering kids away from religion. Again and again, we've faced off over what gets taught, what schools are for, and who gets to decide.

To travel back in time to previous iterations of the school culture wars is to visit a land of striking familiarity. And yet, as we argue in the pages to come, this time it really *is* different. In state after state, culture war is being used as a pretense to privatize schools—or, as influential conservative lawyer and homeschool advocate Michael Farris argued, to "take down the education system as we know it today."[3] Farris is hoping to reach the Supreme Court with an argument that schools' teachings on race and gender are unconstitutional, thus allowing parents to claim billions of tax dollars for private education or home schooling.

Such a decision would cripple public schools in this country, which is precisely the point. Public education that is taxpayer supported, democratically controlled, and universally accessible is central to the American promise of equal opportunity. And as beleaguered as our schools may be—plagued by segregation, underfunding, and teacher shortages—we are a far more equal country than we would be without them. Today's attacks on schools, teachers, and students, then, represent more than just another culture war. They are part of a broader effort to undermine the American commitment to educating every child, no matter their circumstances. They are part of an attack on democracy itself.

The focus of today's education culture wars can seem to shift constantly. Each day brings some new target—a teacher accused of making white students feel guilty, a book deemed pornographic, a school pronoun policy said to violate the religious freedom of conservative parents. Those targets are then amplified into infamy by a media ecosystem designed to provoke outrage. These flare-ups can have real consequences for communities. But there is a greater threat.

Defunding public schools and shifting students into private religious schools—schools where they have no constitutional guarantee of civil rights—will reverse the decades-long push for equality. So will empowering small groups of conservative religious parents to effectively veto the rights, or even the very existence, of LGBTQ students. And at a time when young people are increasingly demanding progressive government interventions in response to the twin crises of economic inequality and climate change, mandating curricula that teach students to accept these threats as a part of the natural order of things is yet another way of slowing progress.

This commitment to undoing what is often referred to as the "rights revolution"—the expansion of civil rights through the twentieth century—can also help to explain the extraordinary role being played by conservative billionaires, both in fanning the flames of the culture wars and in pushing for a school privatization agenda that is guaranteed to make inequality worse. "Equality does not serve the ruling classes well," observed scholar Erik Anderson in a 2023 op-ed. "It never has, which is why the plutocrats lobby so hard against it."[4]

This book is first and foremost about informing ordinary Americans—those who, whatever their political affiliation, care about public education. If public education is going to have a future in this country, they need to understand what's happening in this challenging moment. But if this book is intended to be a guide to the "why" of the education wars, it's also a manual for surviving them.

It isn't enough to know what the motivations are for the present attack on our public schools. We also need to know what to do next. The first step, as we see it, is to begin making a stronger and clearer case for taxpayer-supported, open-enrollment, democratically controlled schools. Perhaps not surprisingly, then, we spend a great deal of time in this book making the case for what public education *can be*. After all, if we're going to fight for the future, we have to believe that it's a future worth fighting for.

1

What's at Stake and Why Should Anyone Care?

In January 2023, the school culture wars officially arrived in Georgia. Inspired by their counterparts in Florida, legislators proposed their own version of the Sunshine State's "Don't Say Gay" law. They had some high-profile assistance in the effort. America First Legal, an organization launched by Stephen Miller—former White House aide to Donald Trump—pledged to spend $9 million on ads and mailers targeting transgender students.

Members of the Georgia Youth Justice Coalition, which represents students across the Peach State, swiftly organized a protest. What they realized, however, was that targeting trans kids was part of a broader political project. The legislators' ultimate aim wasn't merely to roll back the rights of LGBTQ students; it was to advance private school vouchers. As the organization's founder Alex Ames put it, "Republicans were using the issue to try to erode trust in public education in order to justify school privatization."[1]

The student activists responded with what Ames describes as a proactive strategy. They made the case—on the op-ed pages of local papers, through letter-writing campaigns, and in face-to-face meetings with legislators—that Georgia's public schools serve everyone, and that spending an estimated $200 million per year on private school vouchers would rob funding from the vast majority of the state's students. They

Georgia high school and college students rally at the state capitol in March 2023 to advocate for gun safety and school funding legislation. *Credit: Rhea Wunsch*

also talked to as many voters as they could. In Ames's words: "We explained to people that 'hey, this is how much money they're taking from your school and telling you it's because the schools are full of gay kids.'"

Although the GOP playbook of using culture war to justify school privatization has proven successful in state after state, it fell short in Georgia. Both the "Don't Say Gay" bill and the voucher bill went down in defeat, the latter because sixteen rural Republican legislators broke with their party over concerns that privatization would decimate their local schools.

For Ames and her fellow student organizers, the events of 2023 were yet another reminder of the vast disconnect between Republican legislative priorities and what most voters actually care about. "Ordinary Georgians understand that their school is truly theirs—each family pays tax dollars every year, pooled into this shared resource that reflects the community's needs, history, demographics, and yes, politics too," she said. When given the choice to reject their local school or claim it and fight for it, Ames says that Georgians are opting for the former: "The decision to hate your neighbors and reject your public school isn't actually the most affordable, practical, or preferable path for most people."

What's So Great About Public Education Anyway?

Because public education has been around for 150 years, most of us tend to think of it as a natural feature of the landscape. In fact, for many of us, it's a frequent object of scorn: when we talk about schools, we tend to focus on the ways they've disappointed us. Yet the American educational system is something of a marvel. In every community, children as young as four are welcomed into a learning environment that stretches across the full arc of youth. They begin their journeys in school when they are hardly able to tie their shoes and still need naps to make it through the day. And they exit as adults, ready to head off to college or embark on careers. This is true regardless of their parents' race, ethnicity, and income, or whether they have parents at all. It's true regardless of whether those students were born here or were brought here, whether they speak English, or whether they have physical or intellectual disabilities. The doors are open.

The real marvel, however, is that the education they receive is intended to be equal. It isn't merely that they won't be turned away—it's that we broadly expect something between "adequate" and "excellent" in every school and every classroom. "Adequacy" may not sound particularly inspiring. It represents a floor, after all, rather than an aspiration. But look closer and there is a significant set of promises implied by this baseline—about preparation for opportunities beyond high school, training for life in a democracy, and the fulfillment of individual potential. Moreover, Americans have increasingly demanded the latter of those aims—excellence—and have expressed outrage when anything less is presumed sufficient for the children in their community.

> *There is no way that we will ever realize the potential of a multiracial democracy without a public education system that brings young people together.*

To be clear, the principle of equal schooling has never been realized, and any desire we have for real equality of opportunity in the United States will require more than just equal schooling. But pause for a moment to consider the audacity of the vision that every young person should be entitled to a taxpayer-supported education through the end of high school. It wasn't always so.

Once upon a time, public education, if it existed at all, was a charity program. Those with means sent their children to private academies or hired tutors. And if the poor were lucky enough to live in a city with a locally funded educational aid organization, they could send their children to what were known as "pauper schools." These schools provided a bare-bones schooling to needy kids, but they also sent a message to children and their families about the inherent unfairness of society: *This is all you get.*

Early public school advocates argued that something different was needed. Instead of pauper schools, which carried an obvious stigma that often drove families away and relied on charitable contributions that could dry up at any moment, reformers like Horace Mann made the case for public schools that served rich and poor alike. These nineteenth-century "common school" boosters conceived of a system that would serve everyone more or less equally. To ensure the stability of that system, they proposed that it be funded by tax dollars. Schools, in other words, would be less like charity and more like public infrastructure—like roads, parks, and running water.

Of course, the funding of public education has never been truly equitable. Many young people, for instance, were excluded from their states' public education systems for the entirety of the nineteenth century and much of the twentieth—this includes African American students, Mexican American students, students with disabilities, and others. Today, students in low-income communities—in rural America, for instance, or in urban areas without an adequate tax base—often get less funding than their more affluent peers, and usually get less than they should. Still, the gradual shift toward state financing over time has made the funding of public schools even fairer.

Public education can't fix all our social and economic problems by itself. But a more or less universal program that we all pay for and that is open to everyone has resulted in a country that is far more equal than it was in the past or when compared with other countries.

But Does It Work?

Few of us have ever made the case that our local school has too many resources, or that the facilities have gotten a bit posh. One rarely hears the argument that the curriculum is too engaging and relevant, rendering ordinary life a bore by comparison. And we tend not to stand around gossiping about the exciting things teachers are doing in their classrooms. Instead, we observe the gap between what is and what ought to be, and we engage in the great American pastime of complaining about our schools.

There are plenty of reasons why this is the case. But chief among them is the fact that we care tremendously about our schools. That's not just because many of us have our own children enrolled there, but also because we recognize that the next generation of Americans will come out of the schools and take up places in political, social, and economic life. We look to the schools to solve our society's problems, hoping that tomorrow's answers will come from today's students.

Mostly, what we hear isn't good: the nation's schools, we're told, are in trouble. No wonder, then, that in recent Phi Delta Kappa polls, nearly two-thirds of Americans have given the nation's schools a C, D, or F grade.[2]

Yet, our own *direct* experiences with schools tend to be positive. A sizable majority of Americans each year give their own children's schools an A or a B grade, and that held true even through the COVID-19 pandemic. In fact, a Gallup poll conducted in late 2022 found that 80 percent of parents said they were somewhat or completely satisfied with their child's school, up slightly from previous polls.[3]

What's more, there is evidence that suggests we aren't simply deluding ourselves about the quality of our own children's schools. Consider the trends in recent years documented by the National Assessment of Educational Progress (NAEP), often referred to as "the Nation's Report Card." Listening to

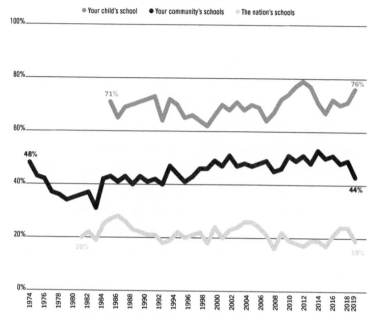

PDK poll of the public's attitudes toward public schools, 2019. *Credit: Phi Delta Kappa International*

the narrative about educational decline, one might expect that student scores on the NAEP had plummeted over the past few decades. But the opposite is the case. Long-term results on the NAEP have held fairly steady across time, rising slowly across the decades. Compared with results from fifty years ago, reading scores are up 12 points among nine-year-olds and 5 points among thirteen-year-olds; math scores are up 22 points among nine-year-olds and 14 points among thirteen-year-olds. Though it's true that the pandemic had an impact on those trends, the overall picture of public school performance is anything but dismal.

In addition to test scores being up, it's also the case that more students stay in school and earn diplomas. In the last decades of the twentieth century, about 70 percent of students graduated from high school. By 2010, that rate was up to 80 percent; today, the number is approaching 90 percent. More students head off to college and earn degrees. And among those who don't, participation in career and technical education offers more opportunity than the vocational programs of prior eras.

Test scores and graduation rates offer a narrow picture of school quality. Yet there are other sources of evidence that corroborate the idea that schools are getting better, not worse. Consider the training required of teachers or the curriculum that they work with in classrooms. For most of U.S. history, teachers received no training at all, and the curriculum was a grab bag—students in the nineteenth century brought to school whatever books they might have in their homes. Even as late as the mid-twentieth century, aspiring educators generally had no student teaching experience and received no preparation for teaching in particular content areas. Today, however, licensure standards—at least in states where they haven't been eroded—require significant pre-service training for would-be teachers, and all fifty states have standards that set a relatively high bar for what students should know and be able to do when they graduate.

Or consider how equitably today's schools serve different kinds of students and different kinds of communities. Well into the twentieth century, a separate curriculum was offered to girls, low-income students, and students of color—a curriculum that emphasized domestic or industrial training. Schools were segregated by race, students with disabilities were mostly turned away, and students not proficient in English were isolated in schools with limited academic opportunities. Rural schools operated with far fewer resources than their urban and suburban counterparts, and the heavy reliance on property taxes ensured that funding inequities persisted across communities even within the same state.

These challenges have not been fully remedied. But our schools are undeniably fairer places to get an education today than they used to be. Decades of activism and advocacy by members of the public have ensured that today's students have rights that guarantee a historically unprecedented level of opportunity. In other words, while there may be miles left to travel, the fight for equal schooling has brought us a long way.

For the past fifty years, we've burdened the schools with an unrealistic expectation: that they will solve the problem of economic inequality. Beginning in the 1970s, Republicans and Democrats alike began to make the case that the primary purpose of education was to prepare people for jobs, and by extension address the nation's deepening wealth gap. Democrats, particularly, advanced this narrative—suggesting that a rising educational tide would lift all boats, and that schooling could expand the middle class without the need for politically challenging projects like wealth redistribution.

The inability of schools to overcome inequality has fueled persistent disappointment with them. As we argue in the next chapter, that cycle of elevated expectations and inevitable disillusionment has left public schools vulnerable to political attack—something that is playing out across the country right now. And yet, when economists try to account for America's economic dominance in the world, and the widening gap between the U.S. and its industrialized peers, they increasingly point to the skills of the American workforce. The U.S.

invests far more in its young people than most other countries
do through public education. While narrowing the purpose
of schooling to job training has undermined the broader civic
purpose of public education, the conventional wisdom that
failing schools are undermining America's economic competitiveness simply isn't true.

Public Education Also Brings Us Together

Public education brings us together by ensuring that, at least
to some extent, our fortunes are bound together. These days,
that's often presented as a bug in the system rather than a feature, with parents being encouraged to care only about their
own children and no one else's. But if we revisit the origins
of public education, the rationale behind a universal system
is clear. Early advocates understood that the only way that
public schools could succeed was if there was broad buy-in.
Instead of so-called pauper schools for the poor and private
tutors for kids whose parents could afford them, "common
schools" (as they were then known) would serve everyone. For
a parallel case, consider Social Security or Medicare—either
could have been offered as a means-tested benefit for the poor.
Instead, both programs were intentionally designed to serve
all Americans, thereby creating a more robust base of support
for programs that might otherwise be subject to the whims of
voter generosity.

Another guiding idea was the notion that publicly funded
schools would give Americans the basic training needed to
participate in their democracy. As scholars like Derek Black
have shown, this idea predated the emergence of a public education system and, in fact, is older than the U.S. Constitution.

Perspective: The Fight for Public Education Is a Fight for a Fairer and More Just Future

By Noliwe Rooks

When you close your eyes and think about public education in the United States, what comes to mind? Is it a shining building on a hill, or a sturdy structure in a beloved neighborhood calling out a welcome to any who cares to enter? Do you see schools as the most direct path leading to an end to poverty and the increased likelihood of familial stability, or how we instill a sense of national belonging in children? Or do you see a crumbling building, unfriendly teachers and administrators, police roaming halls, poised and ready to arrest and harass?

Put simply, I am asking if you most often see public education as a soul-transforming portal to a new life and world, or as a barrier between those with means and those without. Whether my eyes are closed or open, what educational justice looks like to me is the most vulnerable children having the same educational experience as the most privileged children—the same level of careful attention, as well as regular and easy access to the same type and quality of buildings, curriculum, teachers, and disciplinary practices. As I see it, that's what's at stake in the fight for public education. We aren't just fighting for the existence of state-supported schooling, which can be deeply unequal, and which in fact *has been* deeply unequal for most of this nation's history. We are fighting for a fairer and more just future. It won't be achieved simply because we have public schools; but it certainly can't be achieved without them.

Noliwe Rooks is the chair of Africana Studies at Brown University and the author of Cutting School: The Segrenomics of American Education.

Before the Constitutional Convention met in Philadelphia, the Confederation Congress—the legislative body making the nation's laws at the time—passed the Northwest Ordinance, which established rules for creating new states. Requiring the creation of public schools and providing for their funding through the granting of land, the Northwest Ordinance also offered a rationale: "Religion, morality, and knowledge, being necessary to good government and the happiness of mankind, schools and the means of education shall forever be encouraged."

Founders like Washington, Adams, and Jefferson also made the case for public education. In the words of the second president: government has a responsibility to provide education to "every rank and class of people, down to the lowest and the poorest" and a duty to pay for that education at "public expense."[4]

Of course, the huge number of students formally and informally excluded from public schools in the nineteenth and early twentieth centuries made somewhat of a mockery of the idea that Americans' fortunes were linked together. But the push for inclusion increasingly brought the reality of public schooling in line with the high-minded rhetoric that often accompanied it. In the wake of the Civil War, for instance, readmission to the Union required southern states to rewrite their state constitutions—not only to abolish any slavery language and extend the right to vote to African Americans, but also to provide for public education. Over the next century, battles for equal access to education unfolded across the U.S., led by African Americans, Mexican Americans, Native Americans, and others.

In the mid-twentieth century, those who believed that public education could bring Americans together began to make a related argument—that the actual experience of attending school together could foster social unity and coherence. Early advocates of public schooling, like Massachusetts's first secretary of education, Horace Mann, had made this argument in the nineteenth century. As Mann argued in 1848, public schools would instill a spirit of shared community and open what he called "a wider area over which the social feelings will expand." And to some extent that was the case. Most American presidents, for instance, emerged from public schools—a sharp point of contrast with British prime ministers, more than one-third of whom have graduated from the same elite boarding school (Eton College). But the argument for intentional integration across the lines of race and class did not emerge in full force until the civil rights movement.

Residential segregation seriously limited the actual racial and economic diversity of schools. Each classroom hardly looked like a representative snapshot of America. Additionally, formal and informal policies kept many children outside the public schools entirely. But gradual demographic changes, particularly in cities, opened up new possibilities, as did the consolidation of rural school districts, which brought multiple communities together in the same regional school. Although he was writing in dissent from the Supreme Court's 5–4 decision in the 1974 *Milliken v. Bradley* case, which held that districts could not be compelled to redraw their boundaries for the purpose of racial integration, Justice Thurgood Marshall's position—that "unless our children begin to learn together, there is little hope that our people will ever begin to live together"—became a new north star for those seeking to bring Americans together through the schools.

All of this is much harder in an age of polarization and political sorting. When we can't agree on what schools should teach or even what schools are for, a topic we address in the next chapter, the case for an education system that brings kids together gets harder to make. Opponents of the very idea of public education, not to mention the taxes that pay for it, lean hard into the notion that we're now so divided that public schools are no longer possible. This vision suggests that students should attend schools that correspond with their parents' political or religious beliefs. That earlier vision of schools representing our shared fortunes falls away completely in favor of a "choose your own adventure" approach to education that often seems aimed at entrenching political divisions.

Ironically, today's deep divides make the role of schools as places where kids learn together, regardless of background or family belief, more essential than ever. There is no way that we will ever realize the potential of a multiracial democracy without a public education system that brings young people together.

Principles and Practices

It's easy to point to high-minded principles when making the case for public education. You've probably done it yourself, reminding others that public education is a pillar of democracy, or stressing the importance of serving all kids equally at a time when voucher programs empower private schools to turn kids away—because they have a disability, for instance, or because they identify as LGBTQ. These principles are important. The idea of serving children equally, and of extending rights to them that cannot be arbitrarily withdrawn, is powerful. Nowhere else in our society do we make that kind of promise. Similarly, the commitment to advancing the public welfare through education—by preparing all young people for life in a democracy, as well as for productive contributions in their communities—is a principle we should all be seeking to uphold.

But there are also operational characteristics of the public education system that are worth defending, and which are often overlooked. One of those is democratic control. Though it is largely taken for granted, the fact that local schools are publicly governed is an important feature of the educational system in the United States. Local schools belong to local communities. Important decisions often result in community-wide conversations, and though they can be contentious—or even downright hostile—they can also be more immediately responsive to local issues than more distant forms of authority like state offices of education. Local governance also allows communities to adjust and adapt their visions of schooling to account for the range of student needs and goals, and to advance shared community aims.

Consider the beleaguered school board. These days we associate it with shouting matches, but there is a reason why communities that have lost the ability to directly elect their school board representatives fight so hard to get that right back. Yes, school board elections often suffer from abysmal turnout; elected members don't always look like the communities they serve; boards can be dysfunctional. But those are problems to be solved en route to realizing the potential of self-governance. Imagine a world in which there is no public governance of schools. While it might be a simpler world with fewer contentious public meetings, it would also be a less democratic one. Once schools cease to belong to their communities, the case for their existence, including the willingness to pay for them, gets harder to make.

Transparency is another important operational characteristic of U.S. public schools. Take, for instance, the matter of financial management. Americans collectively spend the better part of a trillion dollars each year on the education of students in K-12 public schools. Once you eliminate transparency, the potential for grift and financial abuse becomes enormous. As is quickly becoming evident in states that have introduced sweeping school voucher programs or education savings accounts—the subject of chapter 6—simply handing parents money and telling them to spend it on anything educational doesn't just create opportunities for abuse, it also undermines faith in the very idea of tax-supported schooling. Want to sow a revolt against the largest expense in most state budgets? Make it impossible for the public to see where their tax dollars are going.

Removing education from public oversight also makes young people more vulnerable. Our public schools are subject to a whole host of norms when it comes to reporting allegations of abuse or bullying. Public schools are subject to public record laws and overseen by school boards with open meeting laws, and teachers are required to be licensed. None of this is true of private schools. As high-profile sex abuse scandals at private schools in New England, Missouri, and California have demonstrated, the absence of such oversight can allow abuse to continue for years.

Then there's the nonprofit operation of schools. Americans take it for granted that their schools operate with student and community well-being in mind, and not the fundamental mission of wringing a profit out of the enterprise. Yet for-profit institutions, including virtual schools, charter schools, and "micro-schools," now represent a growing share of the education market. Presently, the idea of making money off students is still a hard sell to most Americans. But what if that were to change?

The academic performance of schools is another example. In the absence of transparency, families might be left in the dark about potential challenges faced by their schools. Schools that can control their own data, by contrast, can always work to present themselves in the best possible light, even if the picture they present is a misleading one. While we may bemoan the outsized and often distorting role played by test scores in defining school quality, students and the public benefit when we have a transparent understanding of what's happening in schools. The future we're tilting toward is one without that kind of transparency about performance.

Finally, we take for granted that our schools are staffed and overseen by professionals. Public school teachers are trained college graduates, as are the administrators tasked with running schools and districts. It may be easy to lampoon bureaucracy or to decry the hurdles that keep many qualified individuals out of classrooms, but a quick look outside our regulated public education system offers real cause for concern. Although it's true that many private schools have talented teachers and skilled administrators, it's also the case that there is no floor to ensure a baseline of competence. For parents to be willing to send their kids to public schools, and for taxpayers to have faith in the schools they're funding, they have to believe in the adults leading the enterprise. The future we're rushing toward is one in which regulation is thrown out the window—posing a threat to school quality, as well as a threat to public confidence.

If We Lose Our Schools, They're Not Coming Back

Two centuries ago, any public schools that existed had little in common with today's schools, at least beyond the fact that they were free to attend. Teachers were mostly untrained, often possessing little education beyond that of the grade level they were teaching. Curricular standards were nonexistent, and what students learned in school was often both rudimentary and relatively arbitrary. The school calendar was about half the length of the current school year, and students would often miss school for long stretches. Many Americans had no access to public schools, and some—particularly those who were enslaved—weren't even permitted to educate themselves at their own expense.

We have come a long way.

America's public schools are far from perfect. Anyone with direct experience can list the things they'd do differently were they in charge. And anyone in a position of leadership will attest to the fact that even being in charge isn't usually enough to institute significant reforms, at least not with anything resembling speed. Yet the problem with America's schools isn't that they are failing; instead, it is that they are slow to change.

Step back and consider why that might be. Providing a first-rate education to every child in a country the size of the United States is a monumental task. Today, 50 million students attend roughly one hundred thousand schools, and are educated by over 3 million teachers. The scale is staggering. Equally ambitious is the breadth of what we seek to do through schooling. Educators are not producing widgets in their classrooms; they are trying to cultivate the development of well-rounded people. For that task there is no quick fix, no simple solution, no "hack."

Imagine trying to start from scratch today. Imagine the political will that would be required to erect a system designed to serve every young person in the country, promising a minimum of twelve years of schooling for each of them. *Every child gets to attend school for free and we'll tax ourselves to pay for it.* Candidates running on such a bold scheme would likely be mocked for promising voters "free stuff" and backing an idea that sounds a lot like socialism. Indeed, as we argue throughout this book, our current school wars are being driven and inflamed by groups and individuals who are outraged over the very existence of public education.

The ferocious push to dismantle public education is not motivated by the failures of our schools, but by the *success* of the project. Our country is a far more equal and democratic place than it would be without public schooling. Efforts to replace public education with a privatized, sectarian, pay-your-own-way model aren't just aimed at schools—they're aimed at the larger vision of equality and multi-ethnic democracy.

2

Why Are We Always Fighting About Schools?

Prayer is out. Comic books and Mao are in. Is it any wonder parents are upset about the "education" their kids are getting? These days the schools teach everything from transcendental meditation to barnyard sex—everything except the basics. Yet parents are still expected to foot the bill. "Trust the Experts," the educationists tell us. "We know what's best for your child."

So proclaimed *Blackboard Tyranny*, an explosive 1978 book authored by conservative activist Connaught Coyne Marshner. A shadowy cabal of "educationists" was experimenting on the nation's children in the name of "equal education," warned Marshner, trampling parental rights in the process. Concerned parents, she wrote, "must learn to go for the jugular."[1]

Some fifty years later, another book would make virtually identical claims. In the best-selling *Battle for the American Mind*, Fox News correspondent Pete Hegseth assails what he calls "government schools" for teaching kids to hate America—all part of a plot by progressives to undermine the family and Western civilization. The solution, he argues, is for parents to abandon the public schools and embrace classical Christian education.

As we argued in the previous chapter, the story of American public education has been one of slow and steady progress over time. And yet the persistent fears over the schools' supposed radicalizing influence—on such issues as evolution, feminism, multiculturalism, and sex education—are also part of that story. The sheer scale of our public education system, the many and often contradictory expectations we have for it, and our deep, unresolved divide over whose voices matter all make schools vulnerable to political attacks. And understanding why such battles have erupted in the past can help us make sense of, and respond to, the school wars that are flaring anew right now.

We Fight over Schools Because It's a Convenient Way to Fight About Other Things

When Americans start fighting over their schools, you can be fairly sure of one thing: it probably isn't really about school.

A giveaway of banned and challenged books organized by the Freedom to Read Project attracted a standing-room-only crowd in Miami, Florida. *Credit: Stefana Farrell*

That's because schools are both national and local in a way that few other things are in the United States. There is one public education system, extending across the entire country. But every American has a local school, often within walking distance. The only other institution that even comes close in this respect is the U.S. Postal Service. But we don't send the nation's 50 million children to the post office for 180 days each year. Nor do we charge USPS with the task of shaping the next generation.

All of this makes schools useful political objects. They allow us to ground intangible concerns—about the pace of social change, for example—in a specific place that is familiar to us. Moreover, schools serve a vulnerable population: most mornings, we drop off children as young as four, knowing that they won't see their parents again until the afternoon. All the way through the end of high school, the vast majority of students in our schools are minors living under a parent or guardian's roof.

Even though most Americans maintain high levels of confidence in their local schools and in their children's teachers, the reality is that most of us don't know what's happening inside of classrooms. Mostly we take it on faith that positive things are unfolding—young people are learning, being cared for, and respected. Yet the door to the school is closed (as well as locked, given the proliferation of gun violence). That makes telling tales about what's happening in schools all too easy.

This mix of characteristics makes schools susceptible to what historian Richard Hofstadter called the "paranoid style" in American politics. As Hofstadter observed in his influential 1964 essay on the topic, paranoid leaders rally support for their political causes by alleging vast conspiracies that threaten cherished ways of living. Their enemies, Hofstadter explained, are "sinister, ubiquitous, powerful, cruel, sensual, luxury-loving." And they possess some sort of particularly potent source of power—they control the media, for instance, or have unlimited funds, or can influence unsophisticated minds. Evil and all-powerful forces are at work corrupting America, and only an all-out defense in the form of political radicalism can stave off annihilation.[2]

Because we generally don't know what is happening in our nation's schools, they are a convenient target for this kind of political messaging. Those seeking to stoke grievance are able to peddle half-truths, distortions, and lies, passing them off as exposé journalism. Although the details change across time periods, the pattern is usually the same. Teachers, they will argue, have become extremists, and children face imminent harm. And it isn't just the children who are at risk: the fate of the nation lies in the balance, since today's students are tomorrow's leaders. Only by rooting out this malignance, those stoking grievance will shout, can we avoid the disastrous fate that otherwise awaits us.

There are examples of such messaging across the twentieth century. Perhaps the most famous involves the teaching of evolution. As historian Adam Laats argues, the anti-evolution movement always had a bigger aim than just keeping a specific scientific theory out of school. "It was instead a confused and confusing effort to make America great again by purging its schools of science, history, and critical thinking."[3] Between 1922 and 1929, a coalition of religious fundamentalists and conservative political allies promoted dozens of anti-evolution bills or resolutions in twenty-one state legislatures.

While the fundamentalists came up short in the 1925 criminal prosecution of high school teacher John T. Scopes—the

Washington, DC, newspaper giving details on the Scopes trial. *The Washington Times*, July 20, 1925. *Chronicling America: Historic American Newspapers. Library of Congress.*

so-called Monkey Trial that pitted Clarence Darrow against William Jennings Bryan—his acquittal only deepened their conviction that atheists were working to drive God out of American life. Redoubling their efforts, conservatives continued to introduce bills like a proposed West Virginia law that would have banned the teaching of "any nefarious matter in our public schools." A similar bill in Florida would have prohibited teaching and textbooks promoting "any theory that denies the existence of God, that denies the divine creation of man, or that teaches atheism or infidelity, or that contains vulgar, obscene, or indecent matter." In short, if we think that the fight over evolution ended when Scopes was acquitted, we're missing the bigger picture.

In the 1930s, educators were once again framed by political opportunists as a threat, but not for their teaching of science. Instead, the problem was "progressive" instruction in the social studies classroom, which critics suggested would "undermine American institutions and prepare the advent in the United States of atheistic totalitarianism." The chief target of ire was Columbia University professor Harold Rugg, whose popular history textbooks were assailed by pro-business groups for seeking "to indoctrinate the pupil with collectivist ideas and to make school teachers indoctrinators of new social doctrine." As a result of numerous book-banning efforts (see sidebar), Rugg's texts quickly went from ubiquitous to unfindable.[4]

Concerns about patriotism didn't end there. During the 1940s and 1950s, the schools were repeatedly accused of serving as seedbeds for communism. Traditionally conservative groups, like the American Legion, made the case that public education was rotting from within. And they were joined by new organizations like the National Council for American Education and the self-proclaimed Guardians of Education, which published pamphlets with titles like "They Want Your Child," "Undermining Our Republic," and "How Red Are the Schools?" Joseph McCarthy, himself—famous for his Communist witch hunts in Washington and Hollywood—announced that he would be "going into the education system" and "exposing Communists and Communist thinkers."[5]

Other school panics of yore feel as though they could be ripped from today's headlines. In the 1970s, Anita Bryant spearheaded a "Save Our Children" campaign that stoked fears about LGBTQ people working with children. Eerily reminiscent of today's anti-LGBTQ rhetoric, the campaign argued that "homosexuals cannot reproduce, so they must recruit. And to freshen their ranks, they must recruit the youth of America."[6] That rhetoric had real consequences, first in Florida, where voters in Dade County repealed a nondiscrimination ordinance, then in other states that had similar ordinances on the books.

Today's efforts to root out "woke" indoctrination from schools are also a warmed-over version of a panic we've seen before. In the 1980s, social conservatives began railing against "secular humanism," warning that schools and textbooks were undermining religion and the family. In one key court case about First Amendment rights in Tennessee—*Mozert v. Hawkins*—parents complained that textbooks promoted objectionable teachings like equal treatment of religions other than Christianity, non-standard family relationships, and the portrayal of women in non-traditional roles.[7]

For the most part, the school wars that have unfolded over the years have been opportunistic in nature. National political fights have been pulled into the schools as a way of making otherwise abstract crusades maximally visceral and immediate. After all, bringing such battles into the schools is, at its core, about stoking fear—that children are at risk.

text continues on p. 35

A Brief History of Book Banning

As long as there have been books in this country, there have been banned books, starting with Thomas Morton's *New English Canaan* in 1637. But banning books in schools first required schools to *have* books.

From the earliest days of schooling in the U.S., students did read books, but mostly they brought them from home. As schooling began to expand in the nineteenth century, entrepreneurs saw opportunity in a growing market. Primers and "spellers" proliferated, as did rudimentary history texts by authors like Samuel Goodrich. Textbooks as we know them only emerged with William Holmes McGuffey's "readers"—all-purpose books that consisted of stories, plays, essays, speeches, and poems. Between 1835 and the first decades of the twentieth century, McGuffey's readers sold as well as the Bible and the dictionary.

School libraries began to grow in the early twentieth century, particularly in urban systems. At the same time, the fledgling textbook industry began expanding rapidly, offering a wider range of choices and texts on specific subjects. With more volumes in the library and a wider range of assigned texts in classrooms, opportunities for outrage also began to grow exponentially.

History textbooks were the first target of book-banning efforts. Historians in the early part of the twentieth century had begun writing more challenging narratives about the nation's past, asking students to consider issues including slavery, income inequality, and gender roles. As some of that newer analysis made its way into textbooks, complaints about indoctrination began to rise. A series of textbooks by Columbia University's Harold Rugg, as mentioned earlier, came in for particular criticism. Rugg's books were banned—and occasionally even burned—across the U.S. by critics who labeled them un-American and subversive.

Book banning reached new heights during the Cold War. As Jack Nelson wrote in *The Censors and the Schools*, nearly a third of state legislatures pursued restrictions on textbooks between 1957 and 1962. Not surprisingly, publishing companies reacted in ways that would prevent their books from being banned. As one writer complained in a 1960 article,

"Many of the textbooks are strangely dull, lifeless, and bear a striking resemblance to each other. Critical of neither the past nor the present, they encourage little respect for the historian's craft. . . . They betray a basic lack of confidence in presenting this country full face because some of the warts may show. Many books present few or no serious problems."[8]

Librarians, for their part, frequently responded to the growing scrutiny of their offerings with self-censorship. "The existence of extremist groups and a press campaigning against certain books and authors," Henry Bach observed, had led librarians to make sure "that there is nothing on their library shelves to complain about."[9] Then, as now, citizens mobilized against book-banning efforts. Still, their chilling effect was real, particularly in communities that didn't have a critical mass of resistors.

Calls to remove books weren't always driven by cultural backlash. In the 1960s, for instance, civil rights groups frequently demanded the removal of racist books from libraries and classrooms. As Bach noted, "The slavocracy of the South . . . insists on indoctrinating Southern children with a flattering representation of slavery and 'Southern values.'"[10] In their challenges to such misrepresentation, civil rights advocates were able to argue successfully that the portrayal of slavery as a mostly beneficent institution was factually wrong.

Most book challenges, by contrast, weren't driven by matters of fact, but rather by a sense of patriotism. As Bach observed, those seeking to ban books "seem to regard as treason any slight suggestion that the United States was ever in the wrong or that there is anything about it that could be improved."[11]

Book-banning efforts were never merely about patriotism. In fact, the most famous effort to limit what students were taught—the effort to restrict instruction about the theory of evolution—was driven by religious conviction. Many of the religiously driven challenges to books during the 1950s and 1960s were folded into broader anti-Communist crusading. It was not uncommon for a book to be charged with being both unpatriotic and ungodly. Even as late as the mid-1970s, groups were opposing texts on the grounds of being "anti-American" and "anti-Christian," as was the case among a group of parents in New York State who demanded the removal of certain books from the Island Trees Union Free School District—a case that eventually reached the Supreme Court.

While it may seem like book banning has come roaring back, it never really went away. According to the American Library Association, the most common reasons for challenging books at the turn of the twenty-first century were matters related to sex or sexual identity, offensive language, themes "unsuitable" for children, and religious issues (usually promoting a religion other than Christianity). Katherine Paterson's 1977 book *Bridge to Terabithia* has stayed in the top 100 banned books since its publication, challenged again and again for blending fantasy with reality, for using profanity (like the word "damn"), and for creating child characters who failed to respect religion.

School Battles Are Often Really About the Expansion of Civil Rights

Political opportunism isn't the only reason we fight over schools. Scratch beneath the surface of our more recent school culture wars and you'll find a common thread: the pace of social change. In the past, just as in the present, reactionary panics about what children were learning and about the alleged undermining of parent rights were also a way of saying "slow down" to social progress, or to roll it back altogether.

Activists regularly focus their rights-based campaigns on children—both because they are in greater need of protection, and because they tend to garner more public sympathy. Moreover, young people themselves are often at the vanguard of social change. As a result, schools have tended to be at the center of the long struggle to make the U.S. a more equal country. But this also means that when backlash ensues, schools are caught in the crossfire.

The civil rights movement is an excellent example of this. As scholars Benjamin Justice and Colin Macleod write, "As the quilters of the social fabric, child by child, community by community, public schools became the prime focus of the movement."[12] Of course, the fight for racial progress occurred across American society—in buses, swimming pools, lunch counters, and factories. But seeking to secure rights in the schools, where federal law could affect the lives of tens of millions of children, promised an unprecedented pace of change. It also produced a ferocious backlash.

Because public schools were a focus of the civil rights movement, they were also a focus of resistance to it. In both the North and the South, opposition to court-ordered desegregation brought decades of fights into the schools. In fact, and as we discuss in chapter 6, it also gave birth to the first school vouchers.

Since then, the push for civil rights has extended beyond race. Roughly two decades after the *Brown v. Board of Education* decision, the rights of two other groups—students with disabilities and students learning English—were enshrined in federal law. In the case of the latter of those groups, significant backlash ensued, and continues through the present. In the twenty-first century, civil rights advocacy also extended to LGBTQ students; predictably, it often produced significant political resistance.

In the years since *Brown*, the legal framework surrounding public schools has continued to evolve. As a consequence, public schools today are arguably *the* key site of civil rights expansion and enforcement. In addition to the Fourteenth Amendment, which guarantees equal protection and due process under the law, students can also appeal to the Department of Education's Office of Civil Rights (OCR), which enforces civil rights related to race, gender, and disability. Moreover, while federal funding makes up a relatively small portion of what we spend on schools, that money comes with important legal strings. In districts where the OCR has found that civil rights abuses have occurred, school district officials must agree to reforms that include educating students and staff to recognize, report, and respond to discrimination. The OCR also has the power to take away funding from states or schools that don't follow the law. In recent years, the number of complaints filed by students and parents has soared, jumping to nineteen thousand between 2021 and 2022 alone, smashing the previous record of sixteen thousand filed in 2016.

While the majority of those complaints came from families of children with disabilities, the spike in complaints also reflects the larger climate of culture war. Seventy years after *Brown v. Board*, we remain enmeshed in a heated debate over civil rights in schools—about who should have them, and about who should get to decide.

School Battles Are Also About Power

There is a high-level conspiracy involving teachers' unions, the president of the United States, and deep-pocketed donors to turn more kids gay and trans. That was the incendiary claim that Colorado Moms for Liberty member Darcy Schoening made during an on-camera interview. When pressed by CNN's Elle Reeve to explain the grand purpose behind what Schoening described as a coordinated, high-level effort, she answered without hesitation: "Because it breaks down the family unit, which breaks down conservative values." Schoening pushed back against the interviewer's charge that she was peddling a conspiracy theory. "It's not a conspiracy theory that the state is taking a stronger and stronger hand in public education and raising our kids," she said.[13]

It would be tempting to dismiss such an outlandish claim out of hand. But similar charges about schools undermining parental rights, presumably in an effort to weaken the family and its authority, have been made by parents for generations. "Even my youngster in kindergarten is telling us where to get off," complained an aggrieved dad in 1924, after the passage of a law mandating compulsory kindergarten. "He won't even eat white bread because he says they tell him at kindergarten that brown is more healthful."[14]

Look back across the decades and you'll find similar battles flaring, receding, and then blazing anew. That's because at the heart of these disputes is another age-old question about government authority in the U.S. and its appropriate limits. Scratch the surface of a showdown over integration, textbooks, Covid masking requirements, or discussions of gender and sexuality, and a familiar question looms large: Who calls the shots over policies that affect children—parents or the state?

That age-old tension reflects the fact that both families and schools transmit values, and they're not necessarily the same. Schools, after all, are where we expect young people to learn to think for themselves, even if that runs counter to the wishes of parents. In the words of legal scholar Jeff Shulman, "This effort may well divide child from parent, not because socialist educators want to indoctrinate children, but because learning to think for oneself is what children do."[15]

The transmission of cultural norms and values to the next

Perspective: Unfinished Democracy

By Jonathan Collins

Has democracy failed education? America's history with public education, since becoming a democracy, has been a story of separate and
unequal—a history of racial segregation, peripheral campuses for
women, advantages for the wealthy, and countless other moral sins that
cut through the very idea of an equitable society. This is not just a moral
concern. We see the empirical realities of test score disparities, of pipe-
lines from schools to prisons, of bodies bullied for their mere existence.
American schooling has seen horror under democracy's watch.

But is the problem that democracy is *inept*, or that democracy is *unfinished*? If we limit the scope of democracy to campaigns and elections,
the answer is likely the former. American elections are complex processes
designed to give the citizenry indirect influence over policies. We select
representatives who are tasked with making policy decisions, and elections become opportunities to evaluate the performance of incumbents or
accept the promises of someone new. Because we choose *people* rather
than *policies*, our influence over education policy is indirect at best.

And then there is the problem of politics. Democracy has been con-
strained by special rules around who can vote, when, and how. It has
been hampered by the influence of money and biases toward wealthy
voters. It has been undermined by the strong arm of partisan politics,
single-issue campaigns, and personal attack ads. Politics has been the
open spew of misinformation and a distraction from the real hardships
that people face.

If we treat democracy as unfinished, we can acknowledge all this while
still moving forward. We can see campaigns and elections as parts of
democracy; but we can also devote attention to other features that should
be more central. Democracy is also about mass assembly and delibera-
tive discussion. As thinkers like John Dewey saw it, it is about collectively

solving our most pressing problems. This view of democracy shifts us from the mindset of "who is right and who is wrong" that plagues electoral politics, to an understanding of democracy as a quest to collectively figure out what is required for our society to progress. True progress hinges on equity. Redesigning schools and districts to better support kids facing structural disadvantages can only happen by sustaining meaningful, student-centered dialogues.

Do our current struggles mean that democracy has failed education? No. It simply means that we haven't yet designed the form of democracy capable of fostering a successful system. We still have time.

Jonathan Collins is an assistant professor of Political Science and Education at Teachers College, Columbia University.

generation is among the key roles that public schools play. But because we can no longer agree on *which* values schools should transmit, that role itself has become the target of ferocious debate. In fact, many on both the left and the right have taken the position that schools shouldn't engage in *any* form of socialization. That poses a major problem for schools, since it's virtually impossible to educate young people without triggering charges of indoctrination. And it's an even larger problem for a society that continues to fracture into disparate camps, replete with their own politics, values, and facts.

Our school culture wars also reflect a particularly American tension between populism and expertise. In prior flare-ups, a familiar set of villains repeatedly emerged—the "educationists," as Connaught Coyne Marshner referred to them: the teachers, administrators, professors, and union leaders who make up the class of professional educators. Today, when parental rights activists and politicians charge the public schools with wanting to usurp the authority of parents, they are drawing on a long tradition of populist outrage about experts who claim to know better than parents.

We Fight About Schools Because That's Where We Place Our Expectations

The system is failing, growing worse year after year, and we're falling behind other countries. Better to just wash our hands of the whole thing and go our separate ways.

You've no doubt heard some version of this argument. In fact, as long as we've had public education in this country, there have been claims that our schools are failing. One reason for that is our unrealistic expectations about what schools can accomplish. As education historian David Labaree points out, "Americans have a long history of pinning their hopes on education as the way to realize compelling social ideals and solve challenging social problems."[16] But with those hopes comes inevitable disappointment when schools fall short.

Scratch beneath the surface of our more recent school culture wars and you'll find a common thread: the pace of social change. In the past, just as in the present, reactionary panics about what children were learning and about the alleged undermining of parent rights were also a way of saying "slow down" to social progress, or to roll it back altogether.

Our contemporary era of school bashing began in earnest with the launch of Sputnik in 1957. Casting about for an explanation for why the Russians were the first to send a satellite into orbit, political leaders landed on an easy target: the schools. The Soviets, they argued, were winning the Space Race because our public education system wasn't keeping pace with the rest of the world.

A quarter-century later, the modern instantiation of the "failing schools" narrative was born. In 1983, the Reagan administration released *A Nation at Risk*—an incendiary report suggesting that "a rising tide of mediocrity" had overtaken our schools. In fact, we now know the commission that authored the report cooked the books. As one commission member wrote four decades later, blaming the schools for any decline in American economic competitiveness, in his view, was "preposterous." At the time, however, the report was a sensation, generating years of political traction. Perhaps even more significantly, it gave rise to a new strategy of decrying the quality of the nation's schools—and then proposing to fix them.

After Reagan's second term in office, George H.W. Bush hit the campaign trail and proudly declared that he would be the nation's first "education president." Once in the White House, he immediately set about making the case that only higher standards could rescue our failing schools. But promising to heal the nation through education reform wasn't simply a Republican tactic. After Bush lost his bid for reelection, Bill Clinton offered an almost identical prescription, insisting that "we must demand more" from the schools. After Clinton, George W. Bush took office and picked up where his predecessors left off—making the case that American schools were failing. Upon signing the No Child Left Behind Act into law, Bush assured Americans that the schools would finally be turned around. Under his leadership, the nation's schools would "be on a new path of reform, and a new path of results."[17]

Such bipartisan rhetoric reached its apotheosis with Barack Obama, who, once in office, made more or less the same argument that American presidents had been making for a quarter-century. "You've got to have radical change," he said in an interview, pointing to America's thousands of "dropout factories" and teachers who "aren't doing a good job." Bemoaning the state of our schools and promising education reforms that would solve a variety of economic and social problems had simply become a part of the presidents' job description.

Of all the problems that public education has been expected to solve, poverty is perhaps the most ambitious—a massive social and economic project that has been dumped at the doorstep of the schools. In turn, resentment about the persistence of income inequality has been directed at the education system. Unlike other industrialized countries that provide families and children with extensive social supports, we largely rely on our schools to play this role. (The expanded Child Tax Credit, the short-lived pandemic-era program that sent monthly checks of up to $300 per child, was a notable exception in this regard.) The view that education is a "passport out of poverty," as Lyndon Johnson insisted, holds deep sway. And even as inequality has grown wider in recent decades, political leaders in both parties have remained insistent that more, or better, education is the answer.

The result of our outsized expectations for what schools can accomplish in this country is outsized disappointment when they fail to deliver. Today, the entire project of free, taxpayer-supported, democratically run public schools hangs in the balance. And yet there is no collective roar of outrage at what we stand to lose—at least not yet. After a half-century in which the rhetoric of school bashing became our lingua franca, finding the language to defend our schools is proving exceptionally difficult.

3

Why Are We Fighting About Schools Now?

Addressing hundreds of parent activists at the 2023 Moms for Liberty National Summit, former president Donald Trump painted a dire portrait of the nation's schools. The educational system, he warned, had been infested by "Marxist lunatics and perverts." To rapturous applause, Trump laid out his plan to "liberate our children" by cutting federal funding to any school pushing "inappropriate racial, sexual, or political content on our children."[1]

Such over-the-top rhetoric is par for the course these days. Ron DeSantis has branded American schools as cesspools of "woke indoctrination." Former Secretary of State Mike Pompeo, briefly a candidate for the presidency, ominously predicted that the "teachers' unions, and the filth that they're teaching our kids," will "take this republic down."[2] Versions of such claims reverberate on the campaign trail and throughout the right-wing media ecosystem—on cable channels, on internet news sites, and in best-selling books.

In the previous chapter, we outlined the various reasons that public schools have so often been the locus of conflict. Today's school culture wars carry distinct echoes of earlier battles over textbooks, sex education, and the teaching of evolution. And yet this time really *is* different. Americans are more divided in their opinions of public schools than in the past—about the purpose of public education, and who should be allowed to

A protester in New Hampshire expresses
opposition to a controversial parental rights
bill. *Credit: Tim Chrysostom*

decide. Education, never a top election issue, has emerged as
the dominant focus of the Republican Party, which sees sow-
ing outrage as an effective strategy for galvanizing voters. The
roaring return of the culture war in the schools has also accelerated the push for school privatization, threatening the very
existence of public education.

Deepening Divides

In the wake of George Floyd's murder and the racial reawak-
ening that followed, school curricula emerged as a pivotal

issue on the right. High-ranking Republicans, including Senate Leader Mitch McConnell, accused Secretary of Education Miguel Cardona of promoting "activist indoctrination" in public education "that fixates solely on past flaws and splits our nation into divided camps." Americans, they wrote, "never decided our children should be taught that our country is inherently evil."[3] That message would quickly become a movement, launching a cascade of laws and new state and local policies aimed at shaping—and limiting—classroom discussions of race and other so-called divisive concepts.

For Iowa teacher Nick Covington, the trouble started in his Advanced Placement history class in 2021. As part of a unit on the rise of European nationalism in the nineteenth century, Covington showed students news footage of the 2017 "Unite the Right" rally in Charlottesville, Virginia, that included protesters chanting "Blood and soil!" and "You will not replace us!" Parents, who perceived Covington as anti-Trump, demanded that the superintendent and the local school board sanction him. In response, school administrators ordered him to stop talking about current events.

While Covington's teaching hadn't changed—he had previously taught the same lesson for three years without incident— the world around him had. Ankeny, Iowa, where he taught for a decade, is deeply divided politically, and the teaching of so-called divisive concepts is now illegal in the state. Covington left the classroom in 2022. Teaching history in the midst of what he calls a "destructive and divisive cultural forever war" was no longer possible.[4]

In Wayne Township, New Jersey, the story was much the same. In 2020, the schools adopted a new mission statement, crafted by a group of parents, teachers, and school counselors, pledging to provide "a culturally responsive, critically

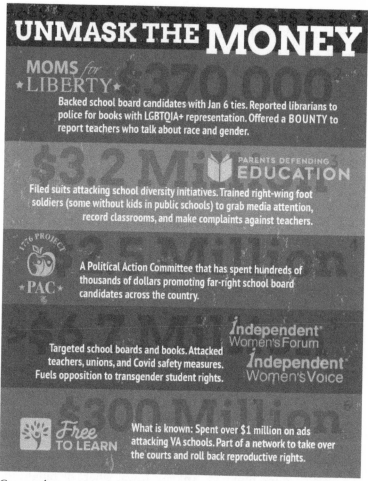

UNMASK THE MONEY

MOMS for ★LIBERTY★

Backed school board candidates with Jan 6 ties. Reported librarians to police for books with LGBTQIA+ representation. Offered a BOUNTY to report teachers who talk about race and gender.

PARENTS DEFENDING EDUCATION

Filed suits attacking school diversity initiatives. Trained right-wing foot soldiers (some without kids in public schools) to grab media attention, record classrooms, and make complaints against teachers.

1776 PROJECT ★PAC★

A Political Action Committee that has spent hundreds of thousands of dollars promoting far-right school board candidates across the country.

Independent Women's Forum / Independent Women's Voice

Targeted school boards and books. Attacked teachers, unions, and Covid safety measures. Fuels opposition to transgender student rights.

Free TO LEARN

What is known: Spent over $1 million on ads attacking VA schools. Part of a network to take over the courts and roll back reproductive rights.

Groups that present themselves as grassroots advocates for parents rights often have huge budgets thanks to dark money donors. Credit: Innosanto Nagara, HEAL Together

engaging curriculum for students of all backgrounds."[5] But the political winds had shifted dramatically since then. In 2022, local voters propelled a slate of conservative candidates onto the school board. The candidates, who ran as proponents of "parental rights," were backed by the 1776 Project PAC, one of a growing number of super PACs aimed at "taking back" the schools from what they characterize as a progressive education establishment. "Activists, scholars, and politicians are currently attempting to socially engineer our society and its relation to race, racism, and power," insisted the 1776 Project PAC. The solution: reforming "our public education system by promoting patriotism and pride in American history."[6]

The fact that we are increasingly divided along political lines, with rival camps of "red" and "blue," is news to no one. But our widening partisan rifts are also threatening the nation's public schools. A 2022 Gallup poll found that a vast gulf now separates Democrats from Republicans when it comes to their faith in public education. While 43 percent of Democrats express confidence in schools, fewer than 10 percent of Republicans hold that view. While public confidence in key institutions, including Congress, the media, and the Supreme Court, has declined across the board in recent years, the size of the opinion divide over schools is unique, and uniquely dangerous.

"Partisan Rifts Widen, Perceptions of School Quality Decline," proclaimed an August 2022 headline in *Education Next*—a Harvard-based education journal. In their analysis of survey data from 2007 to 2022, researchers determined that differences in opinion between political parties were growing larger. Public opinion on current education debates—how schools should handle teaching about race, for example—is also increasingly split along party lines. The neoliberal consensus that characterized education policy for the previous several decades, problematic though it was with its focus on standardized testing, has been replaced by fierce partisanship. Americans are now more likely to support or oppose particular education policies based on their political affiliations.

This deepening political divide has profound implications for the nation's schools. As historian Johann Neem reminds us, our system of taxpayer-funded public schools is dependent upon the support of the entire public, not just the members of one party. "If public education is going to exist, and be truly public," argues Neem, "then all Americans need to be able to see themselves and their interests represented there."[7]

What Are Schools For?

What are schools for? For the previous three decades, the mantra on both the left and the right was "college-and-career readiness." Political leaders and policymakers were also remarkably united on how to measure the success of American schools in achieving this goal: standardized tests in math and reading. Now, however—at a time of skyrocketing higher education costs, and amid concerns among Republicans that colleges are sites of woke indoctrination—the public is beginning to turn against this vision. According to a 2023 poll, respondents ranked college prep near the very bottom of their priorities for schools.[8] And support for standardized testing has plummeted. Polls also suggest that the public has cooled on the central premise of the high-stakes accountability era, rejecting the idea that test scores are the best way to judge the performance of schools, teachers, and students.

The prior neoliberal consensus may have prevented political fighting over the meaning and purpose of education, but it offered a fairly uninspiring vision of what schools are for. Yet even as the bipartisan coalition has collapsed, no coherent vision of why we have schools and what we want them to do has emerged to take its place. Should schools be focused on raising young patriots or instilling religious values, as a loud chorus on the right now demands? Should they be helping students identify challenges in the world, then arming them with the tools they'll need to address them, as proponents of so-called action civics believe? Or is that approach actually Marxism in disguise, as conservative critics allege? Should schools be narrowly focused on "the basics"—reading, writing, and math? Or should they provide students with a far more expansive education? And what about social and emotional skills like self-awareness, self-control, and getting along with others?

Our roiling debate over what we want public education to do is made even more explosive by the contradictory roles that schools play in this country. On the one hand, schools are where the well-to-do launder their privilege. Because most of us presume that we live in a meritocracy, and we view schools as the key mechanism for meritocratic sorting, we accept that those with the highest-status educational credentials deserve the social and economic goodies they end up with. As a consequence, parents are constantly angling for advantage. On the other hand, schools are a massive social welfare program. We all contribute different amounts of tax dollars to the enterprise, and then we spread those dollars in a relatively equal fashion across all young people, even those who aren't yet citizens. Public education, it could be argued, is the most egalitarian thing we do in the U.S.

The upshot is that we're doing two contradictory things at the same time: we're competing against each other in an unfair game, and we're working together to even the playing field. No wonder we're constantly fighting. Any time we don't strike a perfect balance, we're ready to fight.

The "War on Merit"

When Glenn Youngkin won his upset bid to be governor of Virginia in 2021, he leaned hard into the state's school culture wars. Youngkin pledged to ban critical race theory from Virginia classrooms and to put parents in charge of their kids' schooling. To affluent parents who reside in the state's northern suburbs, he broadcast a different message—that Virginia's most elite magnet high school, a feeder school for the Ivy League, had lowered its standards. To these parents, he pledged to roll back changes to the admission process, made in the interest of boosting diversity, in favor of a "merit only" approach.

Youngkin's ability to communicate to two very distinct groups—Republican base voters for whom culture war issues are galvanizing, and affluent suburbanites who see efforts to downplay merit as an obstacle to their own children's opportunities—helped catapult him into the governor's mansion. During his time in office, Youngkin has continued to pound away at the message that a war on merit is underway, including launching a state investigation after Fairfax County Public Schools failed to notify some students that they had received commendations in the National Merit Scholarship competition.

For many well-to-do parents, efforts to address persistent racial and socioeconomic disparities in academic achievement represent a threat to their own children's chances. They are on high alert for any sign that their kids are being handicapped, particularly in the schools. Education, after all, is how young people are supposed to get ahead in a society in which social and economic status are presumably earned by virtue of talent and hard work. This meritocratic myth has turned our schools into high-stakes sorting grounds. Graduate from the right school with the right grades, and your path is secure. Go to the wrong school, or worse yet, fail to get *enough* schooling, and you might just end up where you deserve: at the bottom of the heap. These days, that drop down the economic ladder is particularly steep—the wealth gap is as wide today as it was in the so-called Gilded Age of the late nineteenth century.

For those with a real chance to win, it makes no sense to question the scramble for social mobility. Instead, their energies are best spent moving to the right school district, or even shelling out for private school tuition if it will get their kids an advantage. They'll ensure that their kids gain access to AP and honors courses, assemble gleaming transcripts, and ace their SATs. They'll pay for club sports and music lessons, leverage their contacts, and apply to at least a dozen different colleges and universities. No wonder these folks go wild when local policy talk turns to proposals like "de-tracking" or "open honors." As politicians like Glenn Youngkin have figured out, this education anxiety can also be used for political gain.

Fighting for the Future

In 1961, Max Rafferty, a conservative California educator, delivered a speech that went viral by pre-internet standards. In "The Passing of the Patriot," he took aim at the public schools for no longer teaching patriotism and instead turning teens into "booted, side-burned, ducktailed, unwashed, leather-jacketed slobs."[9] The speech, which was reprinted by *Reader's Digest*, launched Rafferty's political career, propelling him to eight controversial years as California's top education official.

During that time he revoked the credentials of a thousand teachers for being "morally unfit," supported what he termed "a little bit of censorship" in school libraries, and attacked the use of busing to achieve school integration.

Nearly six decades later, Donald Trump channeled the spirit of Max Rafferty in his own broadsides against the schools. Announcing the creation of a commission to further the cause of "patriotic education," Trump denounced what he described as a "twisted web of lies" being taught about systemic racism in America. "Patriotic moms and dads are going to demand that their children are no longer fed hateful lies about this country," Trump declared.[10]

As we argue throughout this book, the concern that public schools and K-12 teachers are radicalizing youngsters has been persistent across the decades. But as young voters have broken decisively in favor of Democrats in recent elections, the rhetoric about indoctrination has reached a newly fevered pitch. The outsized role played by young voters in the 2022 midterm elections, essentially blocking GOP gains, has resulted in calls to raise the voting age and has intensified scrutiny on the schools and what they teach.

After the 2022 midterm elections, Larry Arnn, the influential president of Hillsdale College, warned that urgent measures were called for. Noting that six of ten voters under thirty had supported candidates "committed to less liberty and more expansive bureaucracy," Arnn pointed to public schools as the culprit. "To me this indicates that we are failing to provide kids a proper education—or that others are succeeding in giving them a bad one," he wrote.[11] Hillsdale itself is playing an instrumental role in the effort to reeducate youngsters. Its "1776" curriculum, premised on the idea that "America is an exceptionally good country," has been widely embraced by Republican officials across the country, while its network of Hillsdale classical education charter schools is expanding rapidly.

> *They think you want to indoctrinate their kids, so they've hatched a plan to indoctrinate yours instead.*
>
> —*Colorado investigative reporter Logan Davis*

"They think you want to indoctrinate their kids, so they've hatched a plan to indoctrinate yours instead," is how Colorado investigative reporter Logan Davis describes this mindset.[12] In his reporting, Davis has tried to make sense of the school culture wars in Woodland Park, Colorado, a rural mountain town outside Colorado Springs, where voters narrowly elected a conservative slate of school board members in 2021.

The consequences for the district's eighteen hundred students have been profound. The new leadership moved swiftly to remake the school district, including opening a controversial "classical" charter school that pledges to free students from indoctrination by the left by looking to antiquity for inspiration. Then, in January of 2023, Woodland Park adopted the American Birthright social studies standards—one of a growing body of alternative curricular approaches that emphasizes patriotism and Christianity, and opposes the teaching of current events, civic engagement, and project-based learning.

Over the loud opposition of many parents and teachers, as well as the Colorado Board of Education, which had previously rejected the standards for being ideologically extreme, Woodland Park became the first school district in the country to take up American Birthright. Soon after, a high school social studies teacher was ordered to stop assigning Ta-Nehisi Coates's

Between the World and Me in his elective course because it didn't conform to the town's new social studies standards.

This battle over how to teach social studies in a small school district in Colorado isn't a random one-off; instead, it's the canary in the coal mine—a harbinger of yet another flare-up in a long-running conflict over how to teach history. Conservatives have long expressed fear that if we overemphasize what's negative about American history, students will cease to believe in the country. And yet what's happening in Woodland Park also represents a new, more explicitly partisan thrust to the history wars. As Davis concluded, "It's about turning out the kids to vote for Republicans in 2036—and using taxpayer dollars to do it."[13]

If that sounds far-fetched, consider that the director of Woodland Park's new classical charter school is making that argument himself. In an op-ed in *The Federalist* after the 2022 elections, John Dill bemoaned the amount of money that had been spent (and lost) in the election, urging his compatriots to start conservative charter schools instead. As he put it, "For the price of one set of failed midterm expenditures, the right could teach about 4.8 million kids in schools like ours to think independently and grow in virtue instead of mental and economic dependence."[14]

The Gender Wars

In the spring of 2023, students in Milford, New Hampshire, walked out of school. For months, schools in this southern New Hampshire town had been the focus of acrimonious debate over parental rights, book banning, and policies governing the use of school bathrooms. But when the conservative-dominated school board suddenly limited student access to bathrooms, going so far as to cover urinals with trash bags, more than 150 students left school in protest. The new policy, they said, was demeaning to trans students and disruptive for everyone else.

"I see all these scared people on both sides not knowing what to do yet wanting to help their children in different ways," a sixteen-year-old transgender student at Milford High told the *Boston Globe*. "The best way you can help your children is not discriminating against their peers but listening and helping your child grow. That is all we want."[15]

In an April 2023 interview with the *New York Times*, the head of the American Principles Project, a social conservative advocacy group, made a startling admission. In its effort to find an issue that would galvanize social conservatives, the group had landed on the restriction of transgender rights, particularly among young people, almost by accident. "We knew we needed to find an issue that the candidates were comfortable talking about," said Terry Schilling. "And we threw everything at the wall."[16]

The debate that has roiled the Milford schools reflects the astonishing speed with which new laws and district-level policies targeting trans students have been enacted. Prior to 2020, no states prohibited trans youth from participating in school sports. Today, such laws are on the books in roughly half of the states. A movement that began with a concern about "athletic fairness" now encompasses a broad range of restrictions on trans youth health care and rights.

The bitter battle over transgender rights in schools reflects a deep partisan divide, as well as age-old questions over who gets to make decisions when it comes to young people. And none of this is going away anytime soon. People of younger

Perspective: Should Public Schools Take Sides in the Culture Wars?

By Johann Neem

Opponents of public education have been around for decades. Some are in it for the money: there's a lot of dough to be made if public funding for education can be transformed into profit-generating vouchers. Others believe that parents should choose schools based on their faith and values. So far, these critics of public education have been unsuccessful because, no matter how much they railed against public schools, most Americans from both parties needed *and appreciated* their local schools.

Yet, recently, conservative attacks on public schools and educators have become more vocal and more effective. Most Americans still support their local school, but there is evidence that a growing number of Americans are losing confidence in public education more generally. In many states, legislators have expanded choice programs to help families send their children to private schools. Their success reflects not just long-standing conservative hostility to public schools and, especially, teachers' unions, but also a growing discontent among many voters about the public schools themselves.

This is not just because of Republican attacks, but also because public schools have become more partisan, and Americans are noticing. Debates over American history, critical race theory, and gender and sexuality reflect deeper concerns that the public schools are no longer mainstream American institutions, and that progressive educators—and the professors who prepare them—have embraced an overly critical understanding of American history and culture. In response, Republicans have passed legislation prohibiting teaching "divisive concepts," making it easier to remove books from school libraries, and minimizing the legacies of American racism.

For both sides, the temptation to use public schools to win the culture wars is real. These efforts must be resisted, whether they come from culture warriors on the right or left. Americans want public schools to be places where we confront our failures, but also where we celebrate our successes and foster pride in our country. To retain widespread public support, public schools need to remain nonpartisan institutions.

As citizens we will always argue over what our schools teach, but defenders of public education must be careful not to allow schools and teachers to be perceived as taking sides in America's culture wars. Otherwise, progressive culture warriors may win the schools, only to find that a growing number of American families have left and taken their money with them.

Johann N. Neem is a professor of History at Western Washington University and the author of the book Democracy's Schools: The Rise of Public Education in America.

generations are far more likely to identify as LGBTQ, and be supportive of others who do, than are their older counterparts. That large disparity between generations will continue playing out at the school level as students push for policies that affirm their rights, propelling a backlash that now threatens to limit or even eliminate those rights entirely.

In the previous chapter we explained the unique role that our public schools play in defending and expanding civil rights. Joe Biden has called transgender discrimination the "civil rights issue of our time," and has made the expansion of Title IX, the 1972 civil rights law that prohibits sex discrimination in any education program or activity receiving federal financial assistance, a policy priority. New directives from the Biden administration are aimed at expanding civil rights laws to guarantee protection for LGBTQ students who confront discrimination based on their sexual orientation or gender identity. But that effort has put schools on a collision course with state legislatures in red states actively seeking to limit the rights of transgender students, often in the name of religious freedom or parental rights, the subject of our next chapters.

In Florida, for example, after Ron DeSantis signed the controversial Parental Rights in Education ("Don't Say Gay") bill into law, state education officials directed school districts and charter school governing boards to disregard federal guidance on sexual discrimination and gender identity. Meanwhile, a growing number of states are threatening to reject federal education funds altogether, the bulk of which go to support schools serving students in poverty, in order to avoid compliance with civil rights regulations.

Fanning the Flames

In an opinion piece celebrating the expansion of private school voucher programs in red states, Jay P. Greene and Jason Bedrick, research fellows in the Center for Education Policy at the Heritage Foundation, argued that parents were turning on public schools over values. "Whether it's placing biological males in the girls' bathrooms and locker rooms, calling children by pronouns that differ from their sex behind parents' backs, or teaching a radical and ahistorical ideology that condemns America as irredeemably racist and divides people into 'oppressors' and 'the oppressed,'" wrote Greene and Bedrick, "public schools are breaking faith with the families they are supposed to serve."[17]

It's a familiar argument. Indeed, the Heritage Foundation has been fanning the flames of the school culture wars since its founding a half-century ago. When a bitter conflict over textbooks erupted in Kanawha County, West Virginia, in the 1970s, Heritage seized on the dispute. As one of its publications argued, the public schools were teaching students to "embrace racism, fascism, or any other 'ism,' including cannibalism."[18] Conservative parents "must stop trusting public education," one Heritage Foundation writer implored in 1978, urging them to attack and disrupt their local school boards in any way they could.

The historical parallels are anything but accidental. Then as now, Heritage saw the school culture wars as key to undermining faith in public schools—part of the larger project of advancing private school vouchers. While the specific issues may have changed, the group's goal of ending public education entirely remains the same. Today, Heritage and the network of right-wing advocacy organizations of which it is a part see an unprecedented opportunity to realize this goal. As a result, they're fanning the flames of conflict, and working to advance school privatization policies in state after state.

"Conservatives have never had an opportunity like this on the education issue before," proclaimed Heritage president Kevin Roberts in 2022. "We have to seize it."[19]

4

What's Religion Got to Do with It?

In Oklahoma in 2023, state officials gave the green light to the nation's first religious charter school. Paid for with public funds, the virtual Catholic school has religion embedded into the curriculum and is run "as a genuine instrument of the Church." In Texas, state lawmakers passed a bill that would allow unlicensed religious chaplains to work in mental health

A protester at the Oklahoma State School Board meeting in July 2023 calls for the impeachment of the state's attorney general, an outspoken critic of using state funds for religious education. *Credit: Ashley Daley*

roles. And in Florida, a Christian school that receives more than $1.6 million in state tax dollars each year sent a letter notifying parents that any LGBTQ students would need to leave "immediately."

These stories raise an obvious question: Whatever happened to the separation of church and state?

The short answer is that what most Americans take to be a fundamental tenet of our democracy is under siege as religious conservatives are aggressively pushing their faith into and onto public schools. Such efforts reflect the rising tide of what is often referred to as Christian nationalism—the belief that the United States was founded as a Christian nation, and that its laws and institutions, including its schools, should reflect that. Meanwhile, a string of Supreme Court cases in recent years has demolished previous barriers to public funding of religious schools, giving new energy to a decades-old crusade to return prayer to public schools.

What Is Christian Nationalism?

Christian nationalism is the belief that the United States was founded as an explicitly Christian country, and that the government should take active steps to keep it that way.

- America is a Christian nation, and being Christian is an important part of being truly American;
- U.S. laws should be based on Christian values;
- A retreat from Christian values threatens the survival of the country; and
- God has called Christians to exercise dominion over all areas of American society.

Sources: Christianity Today; Vote Common Good

Keep 'Em Separated

To understand where public schools fit into the church-state divide, we need to revisit a high school civics lesson. The First Amendment to the Constitution prohibits the establishment of an official religion in the U.S. That's because the framers saw the right to a secular government—one that doesn't impose or compel support for a particular religion—as a fundamental right. Constitutional scholar Andrew Seidel puts it this way: "No citizen can have religious freedom when the government can force them to donate to a sect that promises them eternal torture if they happen to exercise that freedom."[1]

State constitutions define the barrier between church and state even more explicitly. And for that we can largely thank Congressman James G. Blaine. A presidential hopeful in the 1870s seeking greater name recognition outside his home state of Maine, Blaine proposed adding a new clause to the First Amendment:

> And no money raised by taxation in any state for the support of public schools, or derived from any public fund therefor, nor any public lands devoted thereto, shall ever be under the control of any religious sect.

What was Blaine up to? His proposed addendum to the Constitution was driven in part by rising hostility to a wave of immigration from Catholic countries including Italy and Ireland. The public schools of the time were full of religion, and students often read the (Protestant) King James Bible during their formal instruction. In response, Catholics started their own schools—the vestiges of which are still with us a century and a half later. Thus, in seeking to ban the use of state funds for religious education, Blaine was certainly thinking about how to keep Catholic schools from receiving public dollars.

Blaine's proposed amendment passed in the House but fell short in the Senate. In the wake of that defeat, however, similar language was adopted in most state constitutions. These "Baby Blaines" *did* effectively establish a separation of church and state in public education. And though initial enthusiasm for such separation was driven by a troubling and pervasive anti-Catholic sentiment, that changed over time, as Americans generally came to believe that religion *in general* didn't belong in public schools. Twentieth-century attempts to peel back state-level Blaine amendments, for instance, were often met by strong public resistance rooted in the idea of non-sectarianism, rather than in any bigotry toward Catholics. Just a decade ago, Florida voters overwhelmingly rejected an effort to repeal that state's prohibition against using state funds to support religious institutions.

As we describe in chapter 6, such state-level bans against publicly funded religious education have long been a source of frustration for school voucher advocates. They have responded by fashioning workarounds, like tax-credit scholarship programs and education savings accounts, that creatively avoid direct funding of religious schools. But as the U.S. Supreme Court embraces an increasingly extreme definition of religious freedom—one that goes beyond allowing state funding of religious education to actually *require* it—it's only a matter of time before state-level "Baby Blaines" are struck down.

Weaponizing Religious Freedom

In 1962, the U.S. Supreme Court handed down a landmark decision on prayer in schools. The specific question before the court in *Engel v. Vitale* had been whether the state of New York could ask students in public schools to begin each day with a brief, nondenominational prayer. The court ruled against the practice, arguing that such a prayer violated the establishment clause of the First Amendment. Yet the matter was anything but settled. As polls found, nearly 80 percent of Americans disagreed with the ruling; many expressed their displeasure by swamping the court with the largest volume of negative mail in its history.

The ban on school prayer, along with another ruling that school-sponsored Bible reading was unconstitutional, fueled a protest movement that would simmer for decades, inspiring an effort to amend the Constitution to allow prayer in public schools. Questions about the appropriate place of religion in a country growing rapidly more diverse would come before the court again and again.

Today's Supreme Court looks at the issue of religious freedom very differently than in the past. The landmark cases of the 1960s and 1970s were based on the First Amendment's establishment clause (i.e., "Congress shall make no law respecting an establishment of religion . . . "). Yet a string of more recent decisions turns that logic on its head, arguing that *not* funding religious institutions violates the Free Exercise Clause (i.e., ". . . or prohibiting the free exercise thereof").

In its 2020 ruling in *Espinoza v. Montana*, the court's conservative majority argued that if Montana was going to allow parents to use private school vouchers to attend secular schools, religious schools had to be eligible, too. Then, in 2022, the court ruled in *Carson v. Makin* that a Maine program sending rural students to private schools couldn't exclude religious schools. In so doing, it marked the first time

Perspective: The Supreme Court Has Opened a Dangerous Door

By Adam Laats

In a sense, the Supreme Court decisions of the 2020s got the history right. When the court decided that public school money could flow to private religious schools and that public school coaches could pray with their students, its justification was that American public schools had historically already been chock-full of religion. And that's true. Sort of.

At the time of the country's founding, it seemed normal to Americans that children would read the Bible and pray in their public schools. It just made sense to most Americans that children needed to learn values as much as they needed to learn to read. And historically, most Americans simply equated morals with Christianity.

So the court had some justification for concluding that the original intentions of the Founding Fathers were to have public schools infused with Christianity.

But in the big picture, the court got it wrong. Yes, there has long been a lot of religion in America's public schools, but it has been guided by a central principle that the court ignored.

It has never been easy for Americans to decide how to include religion in their public schools. From the very beginning, the American solution has been to ban any religious teaching or practice that caused controversy. In the first decades of the 1800s, when America's modern public schools were born, they got rid of any doctrine that would cause fights between Protestant denominations. But as more and more Catholics immigrated to American cities, that was no longer enough.

The battles of the 1840s showed how difficult it is to include religion in public schools. The hard question has never been whether or not to include religion, but which religion to include. In the 1840s, those questions led to deadly riots in cities such as New York and Philadelphia. Mobs burned churches and houses, shooting each other in the streets—all because school boards could not decide whether public schools should include both Catholic and Protestant ideas.

The immediate solution was martial law, but the real solution only came with a widening acceptance of the fact that public schools were no place for controversial religious ideas.

The details kept changing, but the principle remained the same. At first, in the 1810s, it was controversial teaching within Protestant Christianity that was banned. Then, in the 1840s, it was controversial ideas within Christianity in general. By the 1940s, it widened to include controversial ideas between Christianity and other religions. In the 1960s, the Supreme Court recognized that the American principle had to be extended to non-religious students and families as well. By 1963, it was clear: to avoid teaching controversial religious ideas, public schools needed to simply avoid teaching children any religious ideas at all.

There was no way for the government to choose which religion should count as the "real" American religion. In the twentieth century, as in the nineteenth, many of the most ardently religious Americans agreed wholeheartedly. They would never put the government in charge of their children's religious beliefs.

In the early 2020s, the U.S. Supreme Court made an end run around this American tradition. Instead of recognizing the centuries-old tradition of keeping public schools free of any religious idea that could cause controversy, the court crammed a certain sort of religion—the conservative, evangelical Christian sort—back into public schools. We can only hope its ignorance does not lead us all back into the open warfare of an earlier generation.

Adam Laats is a professor of Education and History at Binghamton University, SUNY, and the author of The Other School Reformers: Conservative Activism in American Education, Fundamentalist U: Keeping the Faith in American Higher Education; and Mr. Lancaster's System: The Failed Reform That Created America's Public Schools.

that the court required public funds be used to support religious instruction. Omitting schools from Maine's program just because they are religious or teach "controversial ideas," wrote Chief Justice John Roberts, was "discrimination against religion."

Proponents of state-funded religious education seized on the court's reasoning. In their application to open a religious charter school in Oklahoma, for example, supporters argued that since the state already uses public funds to pay for charter schools, denying a religious school access to that money was a violation of the First Amendment's protection of religious freedom. "Not only may a charter school in Oklahoma be religious," they maintained, "but indeed it would be unlawful to prohibit the operation of such a school."[2]

Such a view remains controversial. Indeed, Oklahoma's own Republican attorney general has spoken out against the school, warning that it "misuses the concept of religious liberty by employing it as a means to justify state-funded religion."[3] But the argument that states must fund religious education is increasingly common on the right, thanks to a dramatic shift in the way that the Supreme Court views the place of religion in our public institutions, including public schools.

When Dinosaurs Walked with Humans

Should taxpayers be required to subsidize private religious schools that teach that the "man is the boss of the woman"?[4] That's the question Justice Stephen Breyer put to his colleagues during oral arguments in *Carson v. Makin*. It's far from a hypothetical question. As historian Adam Laats (see sidebar) argues, the Supreme Court is ushering in a brave new world of publicly funded religious schools, in which tax money is used "to teach kids that dinosaurs walked with humans, that girls primarily come into this world to grow up and bear children, or that only heterosexuals deserve rights."[5]

In many religious schools, the curriculum looks a lot like what it does in the local public schools. Many Catholic schools, for instance, have met the challenge of declining enrollments by keeping their prices low and minimizing religious instruction as a way of appealing to non-Catholic families. Similarly, many elite private schools were initially founded as religious schools, but now appeal to a broad range of well-off families from a range of faiths.

In some religiously affiliated schools, however, the picture is quite different—even if we look only at the roughly five thousand sectarian schools that currently participate in voucher or voucher-like programs. Among those schools, approximately 30 percent use curricular materials provided by Abeka, Bob Jones University (BJU), or Accelerated Christian Education (ACE). And as we know from investigative reporting by journalists like Rebecca Klein, those providers offer a very specific worldview on history, science, and other subjects.

Abeka textbooks, which among the three providers are used in the largest number of schools (including both Christian schools at the heart of *Carson v. Makin*), offer fringe perspectives on history. In the late 1800s, Abeka teaches, Satan hatched "the ideas of evolution, socialism, Marxist socialism (Communism), progressive education, and modern psychology" to undermine American religiosity. "Radical environmentalists," it informs students, "view mankind as the enemy of nature." And Nelson Mandela was a "Marxist agitator" who pushed his country toward "Communist tyranny" and "radical 'affirmative action.'"[6]

Despite Abeka's popularity in taxpayer-supported religious schools and among homeschooling parents, high school courses that rely on their materials are not recognized by a number of colleges and universities, including the entire University of California system. As history professor Kathleen Wellman of Southern Methodist University noted, parents should be aware that although "children might be coming home with a book that looks like an ordinary textbook," the messages inside "are not what people would ordinarily learn."[7]

Abeka, BJU, and ACE also cultivate particular hostility toward other faith groups. As Frances Paterson observed in a 2003 study: "To say that the authors . . . portray Roman Catholicism and non-Western religions in a negative way is to understate the case by several orders of magnitude. All the texts evince a deep hostility to these religions."[8] Reviewing textbooks from BJU and ACE, David Brockman—an expert on world religion and a nonresident scholar for the Religion and Public Policy Program at Rice University's Baker Institute—observed that most Protestant Christians would likely disagree with the theological and historical narratives that the materials presented. "Given the biblical command not to bear false witness," Brockman noted, "I would question whether a distorted history is consistent with Christian teaching."[9]

Precisely how many private schools and homeschooling parents are using conservative Christian textbooks is difficult to judge, but scholars estimate that such materials reach roughly 2 million students each year. And the audience for these resources is likely to grow dramatically as states have no option but to fund religious education.

The Return of School Prayer

A law proposed in Texas in 2023 would have required every public and charter school classroom in the state to display copies of the Ten Commandments "in a size and typeface that is legible to a person with average vision from anywhere in the classroom." As he encouraged his colleagues to approve the bill, its author, rural Republican Phil King, made an increasingly familiar argument: The Supreme Court says it's okay.[10]

King was referring to yet another recent, and highly controversial, ruling: *Kennedy v. Bremerton.* In a 6–3 decision, the court said that high school football coach Joe Kennedy had the right to kneel in prayer at the 50-yard line after each game because he was praying outside his coaching duties—what the justices characterized as a quiet, personal act. But photos of raucous prayers, attended by students from both teams, and testimony from players who declined to participate only to get "harassed and harangued," painted a very different picture. By misrepresenting the actions of the praying coach, the court upended the long-standing principle that states may not coerce individuals into worship. The result: an extreme decision that battered the separation between church and state, emboldening religious conservatives who seek to inject more religion in public life, including public schools.

The bill to require the display of the Ten Commandments in Texas's schools ignited a fierce debate. Public school advocates warned that the measure was an affront to the many non-Christians who attend the state's schools. And while the bill ultimately failed, other measures injecting religion into public schools—including one that allows unlicensed religious chaplains to serve as school counselors—succeeded. Church-state separation, argued conservatives throughout the legislative session, is a "false doctrine."

Emboldened by a Supreme Court that is warm to school prayer, religious conservatives are pushing similar efforts to test the limits of church-state separation across the country. A new law in Kentucky, for instance, allows teachers to share their religious beliefs in schools. The author of the bill, which was co-sponsored by more than half of the Republican-dominated House of Representatives, cited the *Kennedy* decision and said that he hoped the measure would embolden Christian teachers in the classroom. In Oklahoma, the state's top education official recently argued that the state's schools should teach Christian values and beliefs.

Indeed, the question of what kinds of religious expression are allowed in schools has become so confusing that the U.S. Department of Education issued official guidance on the subject in 2023. Requiring prayers is a "no," as is giving preferential treatment to one religion over another. But the guidance also recognized a new reality of blurred boundaries between church and state. "Nothing in the First Amendment," the guidance observed, "converts the public schools into religion-free zones or requires students, teachers, or other school officials to leave their private religious expression behind at the schoolhouse door."[11]

What's the Big Deal?

In recent years, the number of states that pick up the tab for parents who send their kids to religious schools has ballooned. As one red state after another enacted school vouchers, proponents—including many funded by former Secretary of Education Betsy DeVos—regularly crowed about what they called "school choice spring." But we might also call this trend the "season of sectarian education," as taxpayers in these states now have no choice but to pay for religious schooling, no matter how much they might object to the content being taught.

We fund public education with our tax dollars for a reason. Roughly 45 percent of the average American school's funding comes from local sources, and roughly 45 percent from the state; an additional 10 percent, on average, comes from the federal budget. These numbers vary from place to place, but the general rule is that all three levels of government—local, state, and federal—contribute to the cost of public education.

The rationale for this is as simple as it is overlooked: taxpayers benefit from the provision of public schooling, whether or not they have children in the schools. We have a stronger economy, a better society, and a healthier democracy as a result of our free and universal approach to K-12 education.

When it comes to using public funds for religious education, the question to ask isn't whether that is the preference of some families; instead, the question to ask is whether there is broad public benefit in using taxpayer dollars for that purpose. Certainly there is *some* benefit in supporting sectarian education, merely by virtue of the fact that much of daily programming in religious schools isn't about religion. Students are undoubtedly learning to read and write in such schools; they're developing mathematic skills and acquiring a rudimentary understanding of science. But there is also a great deal that we would no longer be able to assume students learn in school, because the matter of curriculum would be left to religious denominations.

A *New York Times* investigation, for example, found that

private yeshiva schools in New York City offer little English and math, and almost no science or history, instead drilling students in Jewish law, prayer, and religion. Yet these schools have received close to $1 billion in public funds. And we only know about the yeshivas' failings because of New York's relatively strict accountability requirements. Other states, including Arizona, Iowa, and Florida, have essentially barred the public from reviewing the content of what students are and aren't learning in voucher schools.

> *The more that publicly funded schools demand that gay students leave, or teach girls that they are lesser than boys, or tell nonbelievers they are going to hell, the more the very idea of public education is eroded. "I don't want my tax dollars going to pay for* that" *is an understandable response to each outrageous revelation.*

Using taxpayer dollars to support religious schools, or any other school that would advance a particular ideology that isn't broadly shared, should raise serious questions for us. Our public schools are often segregated by race and income, given the deeper patterns of segregation in our communities. Still, the vast majority of American children are enrolled in their local public schools, which they attend together, regardless of their religious affiliation. Why would taxpayers support schools with the potential to fracture society even further?

The answer is that they likely won't. The more that publicly funded schools demand that gay students leave, or teach girls that they are lesser than boys, or tell nonbelievers they are going to hell, the more the very idea of public education is eroded. "I don't want my tax dollars going to pay for *that*" is an understandable response to each outrageous revelation.

But the implications of this dramatic shift toward taxpayer-funded sectarian education go well beyond questions of school funding. As Andrew Seidel has argued, the push to expand school vouchers is really about religious privilege. Our current system of "coequal, coextensive human rights" is being radically redefined into a hierarchy in which religious freedom matters most of all. As he writes, "By placing atop the hierarchy of rights the free-exercise rights of conservative Christians, a demographic that is shrinking every day, they can act on those beliefs no matter what the cost to society, our secular government, or the rights of others."[12]

Religious freedom is now being used to justify school vouchers, religious charter schools, and an intensified effort to inject more religion into public schools. But as the separation between church and state is chipped away, the rights of students with a different religion, no religion at all, or whose very identities are judged to be an affront to Christianity hang in the balance.

5

What's Really Behind
the Push for Parental Rights?

Anjene "A.J." Davis co-founded Lowcountry Black Parents Association in 2020 with a clear goal: to help parents in eastern South Carolina navigate the disruption to schooling caused by the Covid pandemic. But his goals for the group went beyond assisting with virtual and hybrid learning. As he saw it, Charleston's schools were struggling in part because of the lack of voice, input, and perspective from Black parents in key decision-making. Give them more say, he argued, and their children would achieve at higher levels.

Yet within months of the group's founding, "parent activism" came to mean something very different in the Palmetto State. In 2021, Davis attended a city council meeting besieged by parents who were furious over mask and vaccine requirements in local schools. Over the ensuing months, their anger would move from Covid-mitigation policies to discussion of race and sexuality in schools, social and emotional learning, and claims of pornographic material in libraries. The activists were whiter and more affluent than the parents he represented, recalled Davis, and they seemed remarkably well-connected politically. Then the former state superintendent of education weighed in, accusing the state's schools of being captive to a liberal agenda.

"That was really alarming," Davis observed. "I think that's

Opponents of a controversial parental rights bill celebrate on the steps of the New Hampshire statehouse after the legislation failed to advance. *Credit: Tim Chrysostom*

when I started to understand that there's something different going on here."[1]

Conservative legislators quickly embraced the mantle of "parents' rights" as they rolled out one proposed law after another: one bill to censor classroom discussion, another to punish teachers and librarians who violated speech bans, and another to create a vast private school voucher program that threatened the very existence of public education in South Carolina.

Lowcountry Black Parents would join forces with a broad, statewide coalition of pro–public education groups to push back against the legislation. In what soon became a familiar exercise, opponents of so-called parents' rights bills would descend on the statehouse, outnumbering proponents. For Davis, there was an important lesson in this specter of small groups of angry parent activists ostensibly driving the state's political agenda offered an important lesson: the power of groups like Moms for Liberty and Parents Defending Education didn't come from numbers, but from the fact that their cause had been picked up by people in power.

As he concluded, "'Parents rights' is being used to advance an unpopular right-wing agenda."

The Original Moms for Liberty

Stoking fears over the supposed erosion of parental rights has been part of the right's political playbook for a century. In the 1920s, stories about children laboring in factories, often at great physical peril, gripped the national consciousness. Yet an effort to introduce a constitutional ban on child labor prompted a fierce backlash in the name of parents' authority over their offspring. Opponents of the proposed amendment, including conservative industry groups like the National Association of Manufacturers, warned that the ban was a way of extending the federal government's reach into the private sanctum of the home. They painted an ominous picture of federal "spies" cracking down on kids helping out on the family farm or around the house—a message that resonated with Americans of all political stripes. Those concerns about the erosion of parents' rights would ultimately help kill the amendment.

Long before members of Moms for Liberty began accusing schools of indoctrinating children, the John Birch Society launched a similar charge. It was the 1960s and the "Birchers"—a far-right organization founded by Massachusetts candy maker Robert Welch—claimed that a far-reaching Communist conspiracy represented an existential threat to the nation, capitalism, and Christianity. Schools were a particular target of the group, which urged members to take over local PTA chapters and run for school board.

Activists, many of whom were women, injected hot-button cultural issues into local debates, including demanding an end to sex education, the removal of "socialist" textbooks and library materials, and the return of school prayer. In communities where Birchers had a significant presence, they often succeeded in hounding out teachers and school officials using campaigns of aggression and intimidation. And even in places where their numbers were few, they understood that a relatively small group of loud, angry voices can still play an enormously disruptive role. Today, the John Birch Society is largely forgotten, but its legacy of culture war, conspiratorial thinking, and chaos lives on in the current generation of far-right education activists.

Anxious and angry parents have also been a potent political force across the decades. The 1970s, '80s, and '90s all saw the "parents' rights" cause emerge as a campaign talking point, as candidates pledged to stand up for parents who felt that the education establishment was infringing on their authority. When populist presidential contender Patrick Buchanan challenged President George H.W. Bush in the 1992 Republican primary, he promised that he would be the president of the parents. "I will shut down the U.S. Department of Education, and parental right will prevail in our public schools again," Buchanan declared on the stump in New Hampshire, a state he would go on to win.[2]

What Rights Do Parents Have?

To make sense of the current push for "parental rights," we need to get clear on what a "right" actually is. Rights, as they are often framed in our public discussion, are absolute—they should be upheld regardless of the desires of others. But most of the rights that we concern ourselves with *aren't* absolute in the real world. That's because one person's exercise of her "rights" runs the very real risk of infringing on the rights of someone else. The right to move one's fist, as the quip goes, ends at someone else's chin. Or, as Milton Friedman himself put it: "Men's freedoms can conflict, and when they do, one man's freedom must be limited to preserve another's."[3] One key role of government, then, is in ensuring that the powerful don't exercise their "rights" at the expense of the weak.

Using this working definition, it seems clear that most of the rights that parents might reasonably lay claim to—at least with regard to overseeing the education of their children—have already been enshrined in the law.

The Supreme Court has weighed in repeatedly on the rights of parents, beginning in 1923 with its decision in *Meyer v. Nebraska*. That case concerned a state law prohibiting instruction in languages other than English—a reaction to World War I and the broader anti-German sentiment that emerged in its wake. Convicted of teaching in German in a Lutheran school, Robert T. Meyer appealed his case, which the Supreme Court eventually took up and overturned in his favor. Noting that the Nebraska law reasonably sought to prevent children from being raised with no understanding of English, the court nevertheless struck it down as an "unwarranted restriction" on what it called "the opportunities of pupils to acquire knowledge" and "the power of parents to control the education of their own." In short, the court found that as long as parental interests did not interfere with the well-being of the child or the legitimate interests of society, those rights should be respected.

Perspective: Five Things to Know About Black Parents' Activism

By Kabria Baumgartner

Since the founding of the United States, public schools have served as a political battleground for civil rights and race. By the early nineteenth century, courageous Black children, parents, teachers, and community members mobilized on multiple fronts, eventually leading what we now call the equal school rights movement. These actions for social change, which emerged in Massachusetts and spread from New England all the way to California, declared that *all* children, regardless of race, had a fundamental right to a quality public education on an equal and inclusive basis. By the twentieth century, when Black Americans continued to be turned away from the voting booth, thrown off public transportation, and relegated to menial jobs, equal school rights became a critical fight in the pursuit for freedom and justice. Their efforts had wide impact, broadening learning opportunities for all children and youth.

Here are five actions from the historic equal school rights movement that extend its legacy today:

Promoting the value of education: Black parents believed in the transformative power of learning and knowledge-seeking, and instilled those convictions in their children and communities. "Improve your time at school" was a common refrain in Black households. Some were so committed that they uprooted their lives, leaving extended family and kin, to relocate to areas where their children could enjoy greater access to schools. For instance, when Oberlin College began admitting students of color in 1835, many Black families settled in northeast Ohio to take advantage of the rare chance to pursue higher education.

Protesting: Black parents organized to transgress and dismantle exclusionary racist policies in public schools across the United States. Their goal was to raise awareness of educational access and enroll Black children in public schools. Group by group, they appealed to school leaders, petitioned school committees, and filed lawsuits on behalf of their children.

Opening learning spaces: In communities where courts ruled against Black children's educational rights, parents continued their work, sometimes establishing alternative sites of education. Educator Elizabeth Thorn Scott Flood traveled with her family from Massachusetts to California in the 1850s, and when a Sacramento public school denied her son admission, she opened a school in her home. Dedicating her life to teaching, she led the local equal school rights campaign in California and later paved the way for the desegregation of Oakland's public schools.

Expanding curricula: Black parents and teachers wanted to deepen and enhance—not limit—course content for the benefit of all children. Wilhelmina Marguerita Crosson, a forward-thinking educator who had studied in Mexico, led Black history school programs in Boston-area public schools in the 1930s. The children in her classes recited the Black national anthem "Lift Every Voice and Sing" alongside "The Star-Spangled Banner." With fellow Black teachers, Crosson integrated immigrant histories into the classroom.

Modeling and practicing democracy: Many Black parents believed that providing children a quality public education made communities better, strengthened society, and fueled democracy. In word and deed, they showed youth *how* to be democratic activists, changemakers, and leaders. And today, these parents continue to seek outstanding and transformative educational experiences that prepare children to be civic-minded and to know themselves and the diverse world they inhabit.

Kabria Baumgartner is Dean's Associate Professor of History and Africana Studies at Northeastern University and the author of In Pursuit of Knowledge: Black Women and Educational Activism in Antebellum America.

Two years later, the court reaffirmed parents' rights in education by striking down an Oregon law that required children to attend public (rather than parochial) schools. In *Pierce v. Society of Sisters*, the court asserted the power of the state to regulate and inspect schools, as well as to require children to attend school for the purpose of advancing "good citizenship" and "public welfare." But once more, the court identified a limit to state power, asserting that the state could not seek to "standardize its children by forcing them to accept instruction from public teachers only." In other words, parents had the right to choose alternative educational options outside the public education system, provided that the basic elements of public interest were being advanced. Children could be compelled to attend school, and schooling could be defined in a particular way; but they could not be kept from being instructed in the family's religious or philosophical beliefs.

Whereas the *Meyer* and *Pierce* cases both allowed parents to opt out of public schools to pursue particular values that might be transmitted through private schools, *Wisconsin v. Yoder* established the right of parents to remove their children from school entirely. Decided half a century after *Meyer*, the *Yoder* case concerned Amish parents who wished to remove their children from school after eighth grade. High school attendance, they argued, was contrary to their religion and way of life, which had been established prior to the advent of public education. Once more, the court recognized the state's compelling interest in universal education. But again, the court reaffirmed the importance of other fundamental rights, "such as those specifically protected by the Free Exercise Clause of the First Amendment and the traditional interest of parents with respect to the religious upbringing of their children."

One final Supreme Court decision, *Troxel v. Granville*, is worth mentioning. Although not directly related to education, the 2000 case examined the scope of parental rights as they applied to other people's visitations with one's children. The

Troxel family in this case petitioned for the right to visit their deceased son's daughters. The girls' mother was opposed to the frequency of those visits, and the Troxels sued. Finding in favor of the mother, the Supreme Court upheld a lower court decision, which had affirmed her right to make decisions concerning the care, custody, and control of her children. Such rights, the court noted, are not absolute: the Constitution permits states to interfere with such rights "to prevent harm or potential harm to the child." But the *Troxel* case once more made it abundantly clear that parents maintain significant control in the upbringing of their children.

U.S. courts have consistently recognized the fundamental role of parents in directing the education of their children. But they have not made absolute declarations about what parents have the *right* to do, regardless of circumstance. The *Meyer*, *Pierce*, and *Yoder* decisions, for instance, all recognized the compelling interest of the state in ensuring the safety and stability of democratic society. And particularly in the *Troxel* case, the court affirmed the importance of the child's well-being as a compelling interest that also needs to be taken into account.

What About Kids' Rights?

"The future plan is to save the country by unifying, educating and empowering parents to defend their parental rights," proclaimed Moms for Liberty co-founder Tiffany Justice in a 2023 interview. "Because if we do not have the right to direct the upbringing of our children, if the government and the state think they know better than a parent for their child, there is no future for America."[4]

Noticeably missing from Justice's statement was any mention of young people themselves. Parental rights advocates typically present their struggle as one against an oppressive state seeking to undercut their authority. But they have little if anything to say about the rights of children, and that's intentional.

Arguing against the relatively theoretical interests of "the state" is fairly easy. Whereas parental love is easy to intuit, and the authority of parents seemingly natural, the very concept of "state interests" is nebulous at best. At worst, talk of "the state" can seem downright nefarious. And history is replete with examples of oppressive governments—regimes that have demanded the subjugation of individual rights.

Of course, we all benefit from having an adequately educated citizenry. That's what is meant by a "compelling state interest." Elections, trial by jury, and many other common features of our democracy depend on a reasonably educated citizenry. In other words, we pay for public schooling with our tax dollars because the stakes for society are simply too high to leave the matter of education to chance. Still, in an argument made up of sound bites, it's hard to offer a snappy comeback to anyone who insists that they "don't co-parent with the government."

Then again, making the case for parents' rights over children's rights is a much more difficult rhetorical trick—especially when framing rights as an all-or-nothing proposition. Often, parental rights advocates will simply assert that the interests of children are always advanced by their parents. Yet there is often a very real tension between what parents want for their children, on the one hand, and, on the other, what would allow those children to think for themselves. Public schools are where young people become autonomous adults, meaning that they are places where youth encounter ideas that may contradict what they're hearing at home. As historian Rick Perlstein argued, "Schools are where future adults receive tools to decide which ideas and practices to embrace and which to reject for themselves."[5]

As we explain in chapter 3, the school culture wars are being driven in part by concerns that young people are shifting left on policy priorities. On a broad range of issues, including LGBTQ rights, economic redistribution, and access to health insurance, young people are far more progressive than their elders, and are rapidly becoming more politically engaged. Limiting what they learn in school, or requiring that they watch videos from PragerU, a conservative advocacy group, in social studies class, is one way to try to shape the thinking of future generations in a more conservative direction. But strengthening the rights of certain parents over their children is another. New policies giving parents more say regarding what their kids can read, or what pronouns they can use at school, are also ways of tapping the brakes on generational change.

Our fights over parental rights also reflect another tension over the extent to which young people should have a voice and a say when it comes to policies that affect them. Young people are increasingly demanding more voice when it comes to such issues as gun violence, climate change, and the rights of LGBTQ youth. Today's parental rights movement represents a backlash to that youth-driven movement.

Other Parents' Rights

In the spring of 2023, parents, teachers, and students showed up in force for a school board meeting in deep-red Hernando

County, Florida. They waited in line for hours to make this point: state laws and directives restricting educators in the name of "parental rights" were hurting students and driving teachers to flee the profession. One of the educators leaving the district was fifth-grade teacher Jenna Barbee, who was investigated by the Florida Department of Education for violating the Parental Rights in Education Act, commonly known as the "Don't Say Gay" law. Barbee's crime: showing a Disney movie that featured an openly gay character.

In recent years, Florida—along with virtually every other red state—has enacted a raft of new laws and policies amplifying the power of some parents while limiting the authority of others. The "Don't Say Gay" law, for example, explicitly gives individual parents the authority to object to specific books and requires school districts to address those complaints, including restricting access for all the kids in a school or even an entire school district. That means that the views of a small minority of parents carry an outsized weight affecting everyone.

As a *Washington Post* investigation found, in the roughly 150 school districts that fielded book challenges between 2021 and 2022, the vast majority originated from just eleven people. If that's a reflection of parental rights in action, then it's a vanishingly small number of parents who have gained those rights. And this trend is on the march. Seven states have now adopted laws that threaten school librarians with jail time and hefty fines for giving kids books deemed "obscene" or "harmful," though what those descriptors mean is left undefined.

New policies governing how schools handle questions of gender identity also let small groups of parents dictate how the children of *other* parents are referred to at school. In Virginia, for example, a model policy governing the treatment of transgender and nonbinary students allows other parents to object to the use of a student's preferred pronouns on the grounds of their First Amendment and religious freedom rights. Justifying this policy, Governor Glenn Youngkin's administration pointed to what it identified as parents' fundamental rights. But a more accurate explanation is that the rights of *certain* parents are being privileged above others.

"They're talking about increasing rights for a very limited number of parents. Other parents who don't agree are losing their rights," argues Julie Womack, the organizing director for the advocacy group Red Wine and Blue, which launched a Freedom to Parent campaign in 2023.[6]

A growing number of states also allow, or even encourage, parents to sue schools, districts, and even individual teachers over policies and materials they object to. In New Hampshire, for instance, a controversial law banning the teaching of "divisive concepts" lets anyone claiming to be "aggrieved" by a suspected violation file a lawsuit against a school or district. Similarly, school officials in Tennessee and Florida can now be sued if a transgender person enters a bathroom or locker room that doesn't correspond with the sex on their official record.

Legal scholar Jon Michaels describes such laws as reflecting a new "white-collar vigilantism," empowering aggrieved parties—including parents—to go after educators and fellow citizens, often financially rewarding them in the process. The stories of such lawsuits then become more fodder for what Michaels calls the "grievance industrial complex," which now powers the right-wing media ecosystem.

The lesson here is that it doesn't take many parents to have an impact on policy, especially when their efforts are backed by deep-pocketed organizations. When a reporter for *Education*

Week looked into parent lawsuits against school districts over pronoun policies, she found that a tight network of conservative Christian groups was behind all of them. What initially looked like a parent-driven revolt over a contentious social issue turned out to be a highly coordinated national effort to restrict the rights of LGBTQ students.

Scholar Maurice Cunningham, an expert in tracking so-called dark money, the vast sums deployed by wealthy interests to fund front groups that attack democratic institutions, especially public education, found a similar pattern when he studied the evolution of Moms for Liberty and Parents Defending Education. Behind positive-sounding names and "kitchen table" origin stories, he found well-funded operations, tightly linked to right-wing networks and conservative donors. What Cunningham didn't find was much acknowledgment of the real education policy positions backed by the groups' funders: "Studies show that the public overwhelmingly disagrees with the education policy choices favored by the wealthy. If the real powers behind the curtain are known, the public will ask questions school privatization advocates don't want to answer."[7]

Backlash to the Backlash

It was November 1996. The Spice Girls were atop the charts and Princess Diana had recently divorced Prince Charles. Meanwhile, Colorado voters were headed to the polls to determine the fate of a proposed amendment to enshrine parental rights into their state constitution. The measure, which had once seemed like a sure thing, ended up being rejected by nearly 60 percent of voters, marking the end of the 1990s-era edition of the parents' rights crusade. What happened? Then as now, parental rights came to be associated with book banning, censorship, and school privatization—causes with little public support.

As Colorado voters prepared to weigh in, a long list of luminaries from both political parties warned that the amendment would unleash a tidal wave of litigation, including against libraries and video stores (remember those?), and that vulnerable kids would be left even more vulnerable. As the debate shifted from the generic rhetoric of parental rights and involvement to specific policy changes backed by conservative parent groups, support for the cause dwindled. The failure of the Colorado effort, part of a national movement to enact parental rights legislation in every state, offers valuable lessons for today.

When Republicans took charge of the U.S. House of Representatives in 2023, a "Parents' Bill of Rights" was one of the party's top priorities. Yet the measure, which included a new federal requirement that parents receive a list of every book in the school library, as well as a notification about the bathrooms used by transgender students, barely squeaked through. Instead of triumphant talk about the GOP being the party of parents, congressional leaders scrambled to distance the bill from the growing push to ban books in the name of parental rights. Virginia Foxx, chair of the Education and Workforce Committee, observed that the bill didn't actually say anything about banning books. And Chip Roy, the Texas firebrand and policy director for the hard-right Freedom Caucus, insisted that the legislation "just ensure[s] that parents know what's in the libraries and what's in the curriculum. It does nothing more."[8]

In New Hampshire, a Parents' Bill of Rights failed in 2023 over concerns that forcing teachers to "out" students to their

After Moms for Liberty rallied around the slogan "I don't co-parent with the government," the grassroots group Red Wine and Blue responded with its own message. *Credit: Red Wine and Blue*

parents could endanger gay and transgender kids in unsupportive homes. The bill would have expanded existing parent rights to include a requirement that school employees notify parents if students were using a nickname or a pronoun that might indicate a gender transition, allowing parents to sue schools or even individual teachers if the law wasn't followed. Linds Jakows, founder of the New Hampshire LGBTQ rights group 603 Equality, says that the bill wasn't really about parental rights at all. "What it really means is control for a certain set of parents to be able to harass school staff and impinge on kids' rights." The silver lining to this storm cloud, Jakows noted, "is that we have so many more parents on our side that see this for what it is: a strategic attempt to divide parents, teachers, and students and undermine the protections that public schools provide."[9]

Four years after parents' rights emerged as a potent political cause, the movement has triggered a powerful backlash. From book banning to the attacks on LGBTQ students, the parental rights crusade is increasingly associated with policies that are deeply unpopular with the public. While the idea of parents having more say over the education of their children sounds appealing in the abstract, letting a small group of parents restrict what all kids can learn or discuss is anathema to a broad cross section of Americans. They see such efforts for what they are: attempts to seize control of the public sphere. It's a distorted version of democracy, in which the loudest voices win.

6

What's So Bad About Funding Students, Not Systems?

Iowa governor Kim Reynolds was triumphant. After multiple failed attempts to enact private school choice legislation in the state, the Republican supermajority in the legislature had at last delivered on the conservative governor's education priority. Surrounded by private school students, Reynolds signed a law that would allow any family to use taxpayer funds for tuition at one of Iowa's private schools, almost all of which are religious. Education freedom had arrived in the Hawkeye State, proclaimed Reynolds. Iowa would be "funding students instead of a system."

That slogan has been everywhere in the aftermath of the pandemic. By 2023, legislators in forty-two states introduced bills enacting new voucher programs or expanding existing ones; in fourteen states, they passed. And every push to allow students to use public money to attend private schools was accompanied by the same rhetoric: *fund students, not systems.*

Separate and Unequal

While the slogan may be fresh, school vouchers have been a priority among conservatives since libertarian economist Milton Friedman first proposed the idea in 1955. Rather than funding local schools and allowing children to attend for free, Friedman argued that the state should send funds directly to

Perspective: "Funding Students, Not Systems" Benefits a Few to the Detriment of Us All

By Jon Hale

Doomscrolling through public education news, posts, and tweets will eventually lead to the slogan "fund students, not systems." It's a popular line. Those in favor of school choice, vouchers, and privatization spin it. They post it, publish it, and circulate it. It surfaces in social media, the news we watch, and the papers we read. It's everywhere, and a lot of followers love it.

It sounds compelling, especially if you don't read beyond the headline. In fact, the idea of funding our beloved children instead of bureaucratic and soulless systems seems like the right thing to do.

But the idea is rotten to the core.

The idea of "funding students" instead of "systems" as we know it today became popular after Black activists desegregated public schools in the South. The racist ideologies that emerged in response, coupled with a lack of political willpower to support public education, decimated a lot of our schools. And it wasn't just in the South. The anti-busing and "forced desegregation" foes like then Delaware senator Joe Biden polluted the landscape of public education. By the 1980s, many wanted to escape the very idea of public education, including some of the activists who committed their lives to improving all our schools. Funding students—not the underfunded, battle-scarred buildings that many conjure up at the thought of "systems"—made sense to many.

The policies behind "fund students, not systems" today are school vouchers and privatization. This is tantamount to using public money to support, if not cover, the costs of attending private schools.

Funding students through vouchers does not and will never help *all* students. School vouchers help a few students attend private schools. And for those who do attend a private school on vouchers, there is no guarantee they will receive a quality education. School vouchers do not cover the cost of the "best" private schools in the nation. In practice, they more often line the pockets of affluent families who already attend private schools.

Vouchers and "funding students only" cause harm in other ways. These policies take money from the students who remain in public schools—the vast majority of children in this country. Many times, those who preach "fund students, not systems" are often connected to anti–critical race theory, anti-LGBTQ initiatives. They propose banning books.

This approach drains resources from children and their schools who need them. It denies wraparound services, including medical support, social services, and mental health. It siphons sources away from social workers, counselors, therapists, and compassionate interventionists.

"Funding students, not systems" benefits a few to the detriment of us all.

Jon Hale is an associate professor of Education Policy, Organization, and Leadership at the University of Illinois, Urbana-Champaign, and the author of The Choice We Face: How Segregation, Race, and Power Have Shaped America's Most Controversial Education Reform Movement.

families in the form of a voucher, encouraging them to enroll their children at the schools of their choosing, public or private. Competition from the private sector, he and his acolytes argued, ultimately would undermine what they deridingly referred to as "government schools."

Friedman's school voucher proposal appeared just a year after the Supreme Court's landmark decision in *Brown v. Board of Education*, which outlawed legal segregation of public schools. For conservative elites in southern states, Friedman's timing couldn't have been more perfect. They seized on the idea of private school vouchers as a way of avoiding court-ordered desegregation.

As historian Steve Suitts has documented, private school enrollment was already on the rise in the South as the threat of school desegregation loomed. But it exploded afterward. By 1965, a decade after the *Brown* decision, there were roughly a million students in southern private schools, nearly all of them white. South Carolina led the charge to dismantle its system of free public schools in favor of a private school system, but virtually every southern state was close behind.

According to Suitts, legislators across the South passed 450 laws and regulations related to school vouchers and tax credits between 1945 and 1965. Their aim: to block, discredit, or evade school desegregation. In Texas, the state's House of Representatives approved a bill that would have given any family that pulled their child out of an integrated school a "tuition grant" to attend a private school, part of a package of bills with a single aim: maintaining racial segregation in Texas's schools.

This history is one that contemporary school choice advocates are not eager to claim. But school choice was born from resistance to school desegregation, as well as to constitutional guarantees of equal treatment and equal opportunity. By seeking to set up a private school system over which the *Brown* decision had no authority, defenders of segregation were attempting to preserve inequality. Today, as red states enact sweeping programs to fund schools that are all but exempt from civil rights protections, it is essential that we recall the original impetus for school vouchers.

An Old Crusade

As we discussed in chapter 4, school vouchers are also a key part of a larger effort by religious conservatives to aggressively push their faith onto students. While vouchers have been rebranded again and again over the decades—from "tax-credit scholarships" to "education savings accounts"—an old crusade lurks beneath the shiny new rhetoric: using tax dollars to pay for religious, and specifically evangelical Christian, education.

But school vouchers are also an ideological project for those whose primary commitment is to free markets, rather than any particular religious faith. As long as public schools continued to be free and private schools were not, the kind of competition envisioned by Milton Friedman was impossible. Yet the vast majority of state constitutions banned the use of public dollars for sectarian schooling, and nearly three-quarters of private schools are religious in nature. Any effort to divert funds to private schools, then, would need to find a way around the law.

Initially, voucher supporters came up with elaborate financial workarounds. In some states, for instance, corporations could receive dollar-for-dollar tax credits for any "donations" they made to private school scholarship funds—funds that would then pay for students to enroll in religious schools. In receiving a tax credit for these donations, corporations were effectively being reimbursed by taxpayers; ultimately it was the state treasury, not the corporate balance sheet, that was depleted of funds. And although contributions went initially to scholarship-granting organizations, they eventually ended up in the accounts of religious schools. Yet, as the creators of such schemes pointed out, taxpayer dollars never traveled directly to religious schools.

Today, as the Supreme Court telegraphs an increasing willingness to dispense with the separation between church and state in the name of "religious freedoms," such workarounds will likely be unnecessary. Instead, even as old policies come draped in new names—like "education freedom accounts"—

they are merely an update on an old and controversial aim: funding private religious schooling with public dollars.

"There's nothing new about this at all," says Pastor Charles F. Johnson, the founder of Pastors for Texas Children, part of a growing chorus of religious groups that opposes school vouchers. "The genius of America is church-state separation. The people who framed our American experiment understood that it's toxic when the government gets into the religion business."[1]

Why on Earth Would We Fund "Systems"?

"System." The word is synonymous with bureaucracy—distant, faceless, impervious to change. By contrast, "student" immediately conjures up a child, perhaps one you know and care about. "I like to envision kids with their backpacks going off to wherever their education is," Betsy DeVos told Fox News in an interview. "And they carry those resources—that money that is invested in them—in that backpack for whatever works for them."[2]

Such rhetoric is now pervasive. In Oklahoma, for example, proponents of the Oklahoma Empowerment Act claimed that the measure was necessary to "ensure that funding FOR students goes TO students—not to systems."[3] The bill ultimately failed, in part because rural legislators opposed it. But top Republicans, including the state's governor, have made clear that "funding students, not systems" remains a legislative priority.

Oklahoma, like every state, has language in its constitution mandating the provision of a system of free public schools. That requirement is spelled out because the responsibility of educating its children is understood to be among the most important jobs that a state has. And yet it has become commonplace to hear voucher advocates rail against such language, as if it is obviously Orwellian in nature. Why?

The answer is simple: because it works. For decades, voucher supporters made a much more straightforward argument. Markets, they argued, were better than democratic politics. Local public schools, then, ought to be forced to compete just like businesses. Families, by extension, should operate more like customers.

As it turns out, however, most Americans happen to like the democratic nature of public education. Many even see it as a cornerstone of our democratic society. With very few exceptions, vouchers were roundly rejected every time they were offered up as a policy proposal.

But voucher supporters have honed their message over the years. Instead of talking about markets, today's proponents tend to couch their case in the language of parental rights, speaking ominously about indoctrination. According to the groups that support vouchers—groups like the American Legislative Exchange Council, Betsy DeVos's American Federation for Children, the Friedman Foundation (now EdChoice), the Cato Institute, and others—systems are unresponsive to children and their families.

Bad Data

When they aren't making abstract arguments about unresponsive systems, voucher advocates generally fall back on a simple claim—that private schools are better than public schools. But is that actually true? Evidence suggests it's not. Student

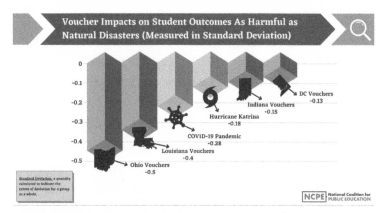

School vouchers have proven as harmful to student achievement as major disasters, including Hurricane Katrina and the COVID-19 pandemic. *Credit: National Coalition for Public Education*

learning growth in public schools, on average, is higher than in private schools. And despite claims to the contrary by voucher advocates, the best research shows that vouchers actually harm the kids who use them. Scholar Josh Cowen has spent much of his career studying the impact of vouchers, and the results he saw led him to become an outspoken critic.

"Although a few tiny studies from the late 1990s and early 2000s showed small gains in test scores for voucher users," Cowen says, "since 2013 the record is dismal." The bigger the program, the worse kids have done, he says, noting that independent studies in Indiana, Louisiana, Ohio, and Washington, DC, have shown impacts on test scores on par with the results following catastrophes like the COVID-19 pandemic and Hurricane Katrina. "If evidence meant anything to education policy, vouchers would have disappeared years ago. But they persisted."[4]

What explains the poor results of voucher programs? While Americans tend to associate private schools with elite, ivy-walled institutions, a more accurate stand-in is a low-budget religious school located in a strip mall or church basement. The bigger that voucher programs get, the more kids end up in *these* kinds of schools. Compared with elite private schools with large endowments and strong academic records, few of which ever agree to accept vouchers, the schools that choose to participate in voucher programs tend to be financially distressed, often taking state money as a taxpayer bailout.

Ironically, even as the evidence mounts that voucher programs actually harm students, the proof that adequately funding school *systems*—the systems that Betsy DeVos and her allies so frequently decry—makes a difference in academic outcomes is now considered indisputable. In states where public school funding declined as a result of the Great Recession, student outcomes declined as well, with spending cuts leading to lower test scores and lower college-going rates. Conversely, as school spending rises, students fare better on a whole range of academic outcomes. What had been a debate is now considered settled: funding systems matters.

The Problem of Scale

There are other reasons why it makes sense to fund systems rather than individual students.

First is the problem of scale that schools face. In the scenario envisioned by voucher advocates, families will be free to choose whatever schooling options they like, coming and going as they please—just as they would in any other domain of the free market. But whereas Starbucks can brew more or less coffee each day, or adjust baristas' schedules to meet demand, schools face a more complicated set of calculations.

Take the typical public school, where class size ranges from twenty to twenty-five students. In a building with four hundred students, that means roughly eighteen classrooms operating simultaneously, requiring at least eighteen professional educators to lead classes of approximately twenty-two students. But when new students enroll or existing students leave, they don't come and go in class-sized groups of twenty-two.

If an elementary school were to lose thirty-five students from one year to the next, for instance, it might lose an average of six students from each grade level. According to the logic of voucher advocates, the school's budget would shrink by $500,000 when those students took their funding allocations to their new schools. But each grade level would shrink only slightly—from sixty-six students to sixty. The most logical move would be to have three classes of twenty instead of three classes of twenty-two, meaning the school still needs the same number of teachers. Moreover, the costs of running buses, keeping the facility clean, heating or cooling the school, and operating the cafeteria all remain fixed.

A school that needs to cut half a million dollars from its budget really has only one place to turn: staffing. Teachers would lose their jobs, class sizes would increase, and the overall culture of the school would be significantly harmed. For many voucher proponents, such an outcome would be a feature rather than a bug. Because roughly 80 percent of school expenditures are on personnel costs, those seeking to limit education spending have long made the case for a shift away from having a trained and licensed teacher in every classroom. No wonder that the same states enacting sweeping private school voucher programs are also loosening the requirements that regulate who can teach. For-profit "micro-schools," which are rapidly spreading across the country, require no teachers at all. Instead, they rely on low-paid "guides" who have passed a minimal background check.

A Fatal Blow

At a forum in Cleveland in 2022, Betsy DeVos laid out her vision for the future of education in vivid detail. Imagining a young man who lives on a large family farm in the rural Dakotas, DeVos described him spending mornings in the bean fields while listening to a book. "He takes his literature courses that way," she observed. He then would head off to an apprenticeship at the John Deere plant. In the afternoon, her rural student would make his way to a charter school where he'd learn core subjects with other students.[5]

Missing from this fantasy was any mention of the local public school, or of a particularly inconvenient fact: rural communities are too sparsely populated to accommodate DeVos's vision of school choice. Even more problematically for voucher supporters like DeVos, in places like rural North and South Dakota, school districts are typically the largest employers and serve as vital cultural anchors, often representing the last remaining piece of public infrastructure. In other words, the "system" *is* the community. Dismantle the schools and the community withers and dies.

For small schools in rural communities, even small declines in enrollment can be fatal. An elementary school with only one class per grade, for instance, can only scale down so much before it becomes a one-room schoolhouse. Schools in places with higher population density are also at risk, as such communities are where new schools—those seeking to tap into voucher money—would be most likely to open. Long known for schools that are too large, urban areas could begin facing the opposite problem: an abundance of very small schools hanging by a financial thread.

Once more, voucher advocates see such an outcome as a benefit rather than a cost. As acolytes of the free market believe, schools *should* go out of business in a functional system—it's a sign that customers are exercising their influence over service providers, and that competition in the market is strong. Students and families whose schools close, of course, may feel differently.

Don't We Already "Fund Students, Not Systems" in Higher Education?

"The idea of funding families directly with public dollars," wrote conservative voucher proponents Lindsey Burke and Corey DeAngelis on the Heritage Foundation website, "should not be controversial." As they observed: "Government officials don't assign Pell Grant–recipient students to colleges."[6]

That's true. Each year, the federal government channels billions of taxpayer dollars to students, rather than systems, in higher education. And no one bats an eye. So, if it works for higher education, why wouldn't it work for K–12 schooling?

If you or your children have attended college, then you know that a key element of our higher education system is that the burden of paying for it rests upon the consumer. In other words, while Pell grants, federal loans, and discounted tuition all help, our market-style approach requires that students and their families pick up the rest of the tab. Colleges and universities set their own prices and then offer students various packages of financial aid—packages that regularly include contributions from students and their families beyond what they can afford. Currently, college graduates carry nearly $2 trillion in student debt.

> *Our experience with higher education funding should teach us that "funding students, not systems" is a risky business. Even public colleges and universities are now unaffordable for many families, whose financial aid packages fail to bring the cost of higher education within reach.*

This is an inherent risk of the model that voucher supporters are peddling. Without a requirement that such vouchers be accepted as full tuition, this approach to funding education always leaves open the possibility that most students will have to pay out of pocket. Indeed, Milton Friedman saw vouchers as a possible route to reducing or even eliminating government funding of education by ensuring that the size of the voucher would remain the same even as schooling grew more costly.

The fact that our approach to higher education shifts costs onto students and their families isn't the only reason that it is a dangerous model for K-12 education. The fierce competition for students among schools also means that institutions often have stronger incentives to recruit new "customers" than they do to educate them. Turning students into customers doesn't force schools to compete on the quality of the education they provide. Instead, they end up selling themselves in whatever way it takes to reach full enrollment. For some schools, that means manipulating rankings in outlets like *U.S. News & World Report*. Others rely on deceptive marketing to attract potential students.

As scholar Nicholas Hillman argues, our higher education system isn't a model—it's a cautionary tale. Instead of investing in colleges and universities themselves, he explains, too many policymakers simply double down on the flawed logic that market forces will somehow improve educational experience. "They won't. Instead, we need policymakers to promote policies that invest directly in colleges so they can deliver high-quality education at low costs to students."[7]

The biggest risk, of course, is posed by a combination of misleading marketing *and* debilitating debt. In recent years, stories of colleges whose degrees are hardly worth the paper they're printed on have become routine. If students graduated from such schools debt-free, that would be one kind of problem—a missed learning opportunity. But students often leave with a pile of loans that can't be discharged, even through bankruptcy.

Our experience with higher education funding should teach us that "funding students, not systems" is a risky business. Even public colleges and universities are now unaffordable for many families, whose financial aid packages fail to bring the cost of higher education within reach. And predatory for-profit institutions continue to prowl the margins, hunting for student tuition dollars. Who do their victims tend to be? African Americans, women, and single parents.

If Vouchers Are So Great, Why Aren't They More Popular?

In 2021, the Club for Growth, a conservative free market group, kicked off its national school choice campaign with a chastening message for supporters. Extensive polling had found that the school choice brand was irreparably damaged, viewed negatively by an overwhelming majority of registered voters who saw choice as "nothing more than school vouchers." Advancing the vision, concluded the pollsters, would require a rebrand. They recommended "education freedom" as a new catchphrase.[8]

Although advocacy groups, including the DeVos-funded group American Federation for Children, routinely release surveys claiming to show overwhelming support for school choice, Americans have almost always rejected private school vouchers when they've been placed on the ballot. In Arizona, voters rejected a universal voucher program by a two-to-one margin, only to see their legislators enact an even more sweeping version of the program. And while political leaders have characterized new voucher laws as a response to public demand, polls show no such thing. Iowans, for example, are broadly opposed to their state's new education savings account program, which allows the use of tax dollars to pay for private religious schools, homeschooling costs, and an array of other education expenses. Democrats and Republicans, men and women, urban and rural dwellers, and parents of all backgrounds express disapproval of the program.

So why aren't vouchers more popular? One reason, as noted earlier in this chapter, is that many Americans intuitively understand the relationship between public education and a functional democracy. Schools are often the most inclusive and democratic institutions in our communities—open to all, governed by locally elected officials, and responsive to local concerns. As such, they are seedbeds of democratic life, at a time when most of our public activity is structured by the free market.

Yet there are also some very pragmatic reasons why vouchers tend to be unpopular. First of all, they tend to be budget busters. States that have enacted universal voucher programs are being saddled with costs that massively exceed projections. That's because publicly funding the cost of education for students who never attended public schools is expensive. Arizona's program, for instance, is on track to cost taxpayers an estimated $1 billion per year—a whopping 1,400 percent higher than what voucher proponents initially predicted. In Florida, the figure could reach as much as $4 billion each year.

A second problem for voucher proponents is the fact that the vast majority of students who use vouchers never attended public schools. Between 70 percent and 90 percent of voucher users in states like Arizona, Missouri, New Hampshire, and Wisconsin were already attending private schools. A similar pattern can be found in states where once-targeted voucher programs are being expanded. In Indiana and Ohio, voucher users are increasingly likely to be white, wealthy, and already enrolled in a private school. As a result, these programs merely drain funding from the public schools attended by the vast majority of students, while offering financial windfalls to private school families.

Vouchers also subsidize taxpayer-funded discrimination. "Let's just stop calling it a 'choice program' and let's call it a private discriminatory education program funded with your tax dollars," civil rights attorney and disability education advocate Jeffrey Spitzer-Resnick told the investigative news outlet *Wisconsin Watch* about that state's voucher program.[9] Reporters found dozens of schools in Wisconsin that appeared to discriminate against LGBTQ students or young people with disabilities, often citing religious principles or a lack of capacity

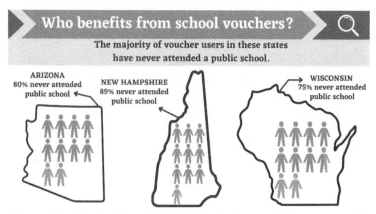

The majority of school voucher recipients in these states never attended public schools. *Credit: National Coalition for Public Education*

to accommodate certain conditions; these same schools relied on public tax dollars for their funding. Investigative journalists in Florida and Arizona have similarly uncovered the ways that voucher schools circumvent anti-discrimination rules.

Yet another problem for vouchers is that they tend to have weak transparency and oversight protections by design. Even as states enact enormous new voucher programs, there are few provisions to track where taxpayer funds are going, or to guard against schools that discriminate, engage in criminal behavior, or fail the kids they serve. Education savings account programs have even less oversight, creating an education ATM that allows parents to spend funds on items including trampoline parks, Disney+ subscriptions, and SeaWorld tickets.

Finally, voucher programs are a disaster for equity. The earliest voucher programs, in Milwaukee and Cleveland, were narrowly targeted at low-income families, most of whom were families of color. No longer. Today's programs are so-called universal vouchers, available to all families no matter how wealthy they are. For states with expansive—and expensive—private school choice programs, it is only a matter of time before the budgetary reality of supporting a parallel education system hits home. The result will be massive cuts to the public schools attended by students who need and deserve the most support.

But We Can Still Choose Public Schools, Can't We?

As Utah legislators debated a controversial voucher program, a prominent school choice lobbyist was caught on tape saying that her goal was to "destroy public education." Allison Sorensen, the executive director of Education Opportunity for Every Child, would later express regret about the remark, describing it as "thoughtless and inappropriate."[10] But Utahans who feared for the future of the Beehive State's public schools were not comforted by the apology. As they heard it, Sorensen was merely saying the quiet part out loud.

Market fundamentalists have worked to convince Americans that they can have it both ways through a system of vouchers. The problem with this vision is that many Americans won't have much interest in paying for an education that doesn't advance our shared interests. Rather than framing public education as a public good, vouchers reposition it as a form of welfare for those with children. As a result, they fragment the broad-based support that was intentionally created by the architects of our public education system.

In a voucher-based system, taxpayer support for education will quickly begin to wither—first for high-income earners, and eventually for anyone living above the poverty line. Soon, we'll be left where we were in most states prior to the so-called common school movement of the nineteenth century. Those

The Revolving Door of Voucher Programs

For most students, private school voucher programs are not a meaningful educational option. In states like Indiana, Louisiana and Wisconsin, roughly 20% of students leave voucher programs each year, either because they give up the payment or because schools push them out. In Florida, where vouchers just expanded, that number is even higher: around 30% per year in pre-expansion data.

Because the typical voucher school is of low quality, often popping up just to receive vouchers, the turnover rate among students is high. *Credit: National Coalition for Public Education*

with means will send their children to private academies or hire tutors, but other consumers will be left with a meager set of options. The poor will be offered the twenty-first-century equivalent of a pauper school—a tablet and an online curriculum.

Though voucher advocates talk endlessly about giving families options, options are not a substitute for rights. That is particularly the case for families that won't readily find options in the free market. Of greatest concern here are students whose basic right to an education requires schools to spend more on services. What happens, for instance, when there are only a handful of students with disabilities in a locality, and none of their "options" can meet their basic needs? What happens when the closest school offering support for English-language learners is fifty miles away?

Proponents of "funding students, not systems" have no answer to questions like these, other than to suggest that supply will inevitably meet demand. Yet sometimes it doesn't, particularly in the case of the least powerful—just look around at the food deserts that drive some communities to do their grocery shopping at dollar stores. Moreover, sometimes what each of us wants as individuals can undermine what would be good for us collectively. We can get what we've asked for, but not what we need.

7

Democracy Is Not a Spectator Sport

The story of the white parents hounding a rural Georgia district's first Diversity, Equity and Inclusion official out of town made national headlines. As a ProPublica report would document, the parents pointed to the hiring of Cecelia Lewis, a former middle school principal, as proof that critical race theory (CRT) was taking over the schools in their district. The ensuing outrage would lead Lewis to quit the job she had yet to start, providing shameful proof of the potency of the school culture wars.

What happened next got far less attention. When those same parents ran for school board in 2022—united as a self-proclaimed "family values" slate and backed by the national 1776 Project PAC—they failed to pick up a single seat. Their opposition to equity plans and their claims that the local schools were indoctrinating students through district-provided Chromebooks fell flat with local voters. But it was likely their embrace of school privatization that did the candidates in. Arguments in favor of vouchers landed with a thud in a rural county where the closest private schools are sixty miles away. Anti–public school messaging, including arguments that local businesses shouldn't have to pay taxes to support the local schools, fared no better.

"These were wildly unpopular positions," says Alex Ames, founder of the Georgia Youth Justice Coalition. Voters who may have been supportive of the initial effort to "take back the schools" revolted at the idea of defunding them. As Ames put it: "You started to hear people say things like, 'Wait a second. My daughter has a disability and she goes to that school.' Opposition really started to steamroll once people understood that this was about taking something away from them."[1]

What happened in Georgia isn't unique. While groups like Moms for Liberty have excelled at generating news coverage, culture war candidates have not fared particularly well at the ballot box. Indeed, Glenn Youngkin's upset gubernatorial win in Virginia looks, in retrospect, more like an outlier than a bellwether. The parental rights cause may have rallied the base, but it hasn't attracted independents or won back the "suburban mom" vote that the GOP lost during the Trump era.

It turns out that most people don't want someone else's parents or some outside group telling their kids what they can read or what ideas they can consider.

—David Pepper, author, Laboratories of Autocracy

According to Ballotpedia, a site that tracks U.S. elections, in nearly 1,800 school board races across the country, conservative candidates who opposed discussions of race or gender in classrooms, or opposed mask mandates during the pandemic, lost 70 percent of their races. Even in states where lawmakers have aggressively pursued culture war agendas, including limits on discussions of race or gender in schools, candidates who have embraced the same themes often fall short when local voters have a choice.

In Ohio, for instance, far-right candidates for school board popped up across the state in 2021, running on opposition to vaccines and CRT. Yet as political observer David Pepper notes, most of those candidates ended up losing, even in deeply red parts of the state. A similar dynamic played out in school board races in the Buckeye State in 2022 and 2023. How, then, can we explain the fact that local voters are saying no to these candidates at a time when the state board of education and state lawmakers have relentlessly focused on culture war issues? Pepper, a veteran of Ohio politics and the author of *Laboratories of Autocracy*, points to the fact that school board races aren't gerrymandered, making them among the rare red state contests that aren't predetermined.

But failures of culture war candidates also reflect the fact that the cause of parental rights is increasingly associated with policies that majorities of Americans reject, including censorship and book banning. As Pepper put it: "It turns out that most people don't want someone else's parents or some outside group telling their kids what they can read or what ideas they can consider."[2]

When the advocacy group Moms Rising polled its members in 2023, it found that parents across the political spectrum shared a set of common concerns, including affordable child care, safe schools, and gun safety as their top concerns. What the group's million-plus members *didn't* care about was the constellation of policy positions that co-founder Kristin Rowe-Finkbeiner characterizes as "hate spaghetti"—book bans, the exclusion of LGBTQ students, and efforts to whitewash history. "Well-funded groups are throwing issue after issue at the wall to see what sticks," she observed. But while "hate is twice as sticky," Rowe-Finkbeiner is persuaded that such messages ultimately have no staying power. "Moms are waking up and are beginning to understand that this is a political campaign aimed at tearing us apart."[3]

Anger and Resolve

Laura Leigh Abby was shocked when she saw the signs. A candidate for school board in her Hudson Valley, New York, community was trumpeting "Christ Is King" on his placards, pledging to "end the sexualization of children" in the local schools. Abby, who is married to her same-sex partner and has two young children, learned that he was just one of a group of candidates affiliated with the local chapter of Moms for Liberty. "Anti-LGBTQ and anti-trans legislation is alarming, but groups like these are attacking our families on a much smaller scale, right in our own neighborhoods," she wrote in a 2022 essay.[4]

Fear gave way to anger and then to resolve. Abby joined with other concerned parents to mobilize against the candidates, making the case to local voters that "Teachers Shouldn't Be Preachers" and urging them to vote in the upcoming election. All three of the candidates endorsed by Moms for Liberty ended up losing in a contest that saw double the usual voter turnout. But Abby was just getting started. She and parent Karen Svoboda went on to found Defense of Democracy, which offers training and assistance to parents and other public school advocates seeking to start groups of their own.

Hundreds of groups are now pushing back against campaigns to ban books, inject religion into curriculum, and defund public schools. While these efforts are often grassroots and small-scale, a number of organizations—groups including Defense of Democracy, Red Wine and Blue, and HEAL Together—are increasingly providing national coordination, sharing tips about how to effectively rally local communities around a vision of fully funded public schools that serve all kids.

Karin Chenoweth spent her career as an education journalist documenting success stories in school districts that serve high numbers of low-income and racially minoritized students. But by 2021, she was following with mounting concern the stories of extremist school board candidates, and the deep-pocketed groups that were fanning the flames of school culture wars. "The stakes are clear: they want to destroy public education," concluded Chenoweth. "There's a whole playbook."[5]

Chenoweth started Democracy and Education with the aim of bringing together those seeking to protect public education. Today, she is one of a growing number of experts on what it takes to defeat extremists at the local level, as well as on why it remains so urgent to do just that. In places where such candidates have been victorious, says Chenoweth, they have done enormous damage, and often in a short period of time. "They harass and intimidate staff; they ban books; they charter religious schools. They do all kinds of things that most Americans don't want." But in communities that organize to rally the majority, extremists are almost always defeated. "It takes work, organization, and dedication on the part of ordinary citizens—which is how democracy is supposed to work," notes Chenoweth. "The old saying is, 'Democracy is not a spectator sport,' and the fight over school boards demonstrates exactly how true that is."

A Popular Vision

In 2023, the Popular Comms Institute in Lancaster, Pennsylvania, conducted a research study with more than three thousand respondents across five battleground states. The goal: to identify which messages would be most effective in defending public education and defeating authoritarian rhetoric. On four different issues—public education, critical race theory, book bans, and transgender student athletes—the group tested what they described as "authoritarian messaging" against rhetoric that was inclusive and pro–public education. It found that on every issue, a positive vision for making public education stronger and investing in kids outperformed authoritarian messages, regardless of factors like voter age, race, and education. And while such messaging was especially popular with Democrats, it also strongly resonated with independents and Republicans.

Popular Comms concluded that the most effective strategy for defending public schools from extremist attacks was to tell a "Big Us, Small Them" story. Such messaging starts by telling a story of shared values about what kids in a given community deserve, and invoking a multiracial "us" that is bigger than "them." The strategy does include responding to divisive rhetoric, as well as calling out the deep-pocketed donors and ideologically aligned organizations that are often behind culture war flare-ups at the local level. But the power of "Big Us, Small Them" messaging comes from the breadth of the positive vision being put forward.

"Our positive vision for public education is popular and our opponents know it," says Popular Comms co-founder Allison Troy. "That's why they keep manufacturing new ways to sow fear and hate in order to divide us against each other and distract us." For Troy, their study offered decisive evidence that people prefer a vision of abundance and possibility for kids—one that includes investment in public education. "Our

opponents know the only way they can win is through divi-
sion," Troy observed. "We win by coming together around a
clearly articulated vision of the future where every child in
every community gets what they need to thrive at school."[6]

Other groups have learned the same lesson: that playing
defense isn't sufficient to counter extremism. "It isn't enough
to just push back," says Zandra Rice Hawkins, executive
director of Granite State Progress, which works with school
board candidates across New Hampshire. "In places that are
successfully defeating the right's agenda it's because all sorts of
groups and people are coming together to talk about what they
want their community to look like."[7]

Candidates in New Hampshire who have run on dismantling
public education, censoring history, and targeting LGBTQ students and their families have now gone down to defeat across
multiple election cycles. Even in the most conservative parts
of the state, voters are regularly rejecting culture war candidates. In fact, New Hampshire's transformation from a solid-
red GOP bastion to an occasionally left-leaning purple state
has been driven in part by the backlash against an extreme
education agenda. Rice Hawkins points to a recent vote in
Wolfeboro, New Hampshire—long considered a Republican
stronghold—where locals voted by a wide margin to prohibit "the banning of books or any other content from our
Wolfeboro Public Library, thereby guaranteeing our citizens
their First Amendment Rights and their rights under the New
Hampshire Constitution." The issue prompted a local reckon-
ing over the town's identity, says Rice Hawkins. "Once the
discussion turns to 'what kind of community do we want to
be?' the answer is almost always bigger and more inclusive
than what the right is offering."

Party-Free Zone

At a time of bitter partisan rancor, coalitions coming together in support of public education frequently transcend political divides. That's because the vast majority of states still require nonpartisan school board races—the legacy of historical efforts to keep politics out of public education. And although lawmakers in multiple states have proposed making school board races partisan, which tends to help Republican candidates, their efforts have found little public support. In Indiana, for example, a high-profile effort to require party identifiers on school board election ballots died in committee after not a single person testified in favor of the switch.

Despite all the rhetoric from the right regarding public schools as sites of political indoctrination, most Americans still see public education as a nonpartisan issue. That creates an opening for political candidates and coalitions of public school advocates to appeal to voters in ways that don't simply reflect party orthodoxies.

Of course, avoiding partisanship can also be a challenge, especially when extreme candidates and organizations tout their political allegiances. Some have wondered if it might be politically savvy to make defending public education a priority of the Democratic Party. Yet the danger in doing so is that partisan framing of education issues risks alienating voters who are in what Zandra Rice Hawkins describes as the movable middle. "They're hearing a lot of noise about book bans and bathroom policies from the right. Our challenge is to figure out how to talk about these issues and why they matter without politicizing them."

In communities where extremist candidates and issue

campaigns have been defeated, it's not because the left beat
back the right, says Rice Hawkins. Rather, it's because a broad
swathe of voters came together in support of shared values—
the belief that all kids deserve access to high-quality education, for instance, or that a community cares about *all* of its
kids. "We end up outnumbering the right every time."

Finding Common Ground

When Heather DuBois Bourenane, the executive director of
the Wisconsin Public Education Network, speaks to school
administrators, she comes bearing what sounds like surpris-
ing advice: *Your angriest parent can be your greatest ally.* The
prospect of finding common ground with parents outraged
over an ever-growing list of targets can seem daunting, even
naive. But it's a challenge that DuBois Bourenane and her fellow public school advocates eagerly embrace. "The people
who are motivated to seek change are the people who are the
most worked up, even if they're mad for the wrong reasons.
They've already proven to you that they're willing to take the
first step."[8]

In exchanges with parents who are worried about indoctrination, DuBois Bourenane doesn't respond with facts about
what is and isn't happening in the local schools. Instead, she
asks these parents what it would look like if their children
were getting the best possible education. The answers are illu-
minating, she says. "They want schools that are fully funded
and staffed by adults who care about their kids and recognize them. There's the common ground." The next step in
the conversation entails what DuBois Bourenane describes as
connecting the dots, helping parents see that the gap between

what they want and what their school currently provides is the result of years of intentional underfunding by Wisconsin's GOP-controlled legislature.

The strategy doesn't always work, she acknowledges. Sometimes the anger is too intense or the distance in values too great to overcome. But the exercise is always worthwhile. "Even if you can't find a shared value, understanding where they're coming from makes you better," says DuBois Bourenane.

According to the Popular Comms Institute, these messaging strategies are among the least effective for defending public education:

Counter-arguments that try to prove the other side wrong
Critical race theory is a grad school–level legal framework. It isn't taught in our schools. Chances are you've heard this claim made, or even made it yourself. Yet so-called counter-argument messaging is the least effective, in part because it often includes specialized terminology and jargon that can come across as condescending.

Condescending rhetoric that belittles other parents
Avoid rhetoric that characterizes other parents as ignorant, or portrays them as lacking in agency.

Overreliance on facts and data
This approach can also play into the characterization of public school advocates as arrogant elitists.

Presenting vulnerable students as victims
No matter how well intentioned, portraying vulnerable students solely as victims is counter-productive. The solution: allow students to tell their own stories as part of a larger vision of what the community values.

Defending Public Schools Doesn't Mean Defending the Status Quo

When organizers of Public School Strong in North Carolina ask parents and teachers to envision what the state's privatization trajectory will mean for students and the schools they attend, they describe a world of sharp divides. It's not hard for them to picture more affluent parents fleeing to white-flight charter schools and private schools, leaving behind gutted public schools, says Public School Strong coordinator Isabell Moore. "They say that Black and Brown students and working-class students are going to have the most bare-bones education, without the resources they need."[9]

Public School Strong, which now counts active members in two-thirds of North Carolina's counties, emerged to oppose the sweeping expansion of the Tar Heel State's private school voucher program and the diversion of tax dollars away from public schools. But while advocates see themselves as defending public schools, what they're not defending is the status quo—the state's long history of unequal education and racial segregation.

"We recognize that public education is a public good, but we also recognize that our schools haven't been perfect for our families and that they need to be transformed," says Letha Muhammad, executive director of the Education Justice Alliance in Raleigh, North Carolina, which is part of a growing pro–public education coalition known as HEAL Together NC.[10] That coalition has embraced the urgent mission of protecting the Tar Heel State's public schools while also acknowledging that far too many of North Carolina's children fail to get

Local Public School Strong members in Mecklenburg County, North Carolina. *Credit: Public School Strong*

the resources they need. Transforming the schools would mean ensuring that every child in the state gets the equal opportunities promised in the state's constitution—opportunities that have yet to be delivered upon.

While bringing together parents with radically different experiences in the public education system can make for challenging organizing, Moore admits, members of the HEAL Together NC coalition are convinced that the strategy will pay off. "When we can come together across lines of difference and say, 'We want to defend and protect these schools, and we want to make them better for all our families and all our communities,' we think we can turn the tide."

It Takes More Than One Group of People

Even in strongly Republican Roanoke County, Virginia, the 2021 school board election represented a new extreme. Candidates for the nonpartisan positions touted their culture war credentials and endorsements from the state's GOP governor. And once elected, the new board members quickly set about translating their parental rights rhetoric into policy. Over the past two years, the board has adopted one divisive measure after another, including policies marginalizing LGBTQ students and a ban on any classroom displays that reflect the personal views of teachers.

The board's agenda has also spawned a strong community response. A growing coalition, the Roanoke County Collaborative for Schools Our Students Deserve, has come together in opposition to the religious and ideological tenor of the board's policy direction. "People are coming together to say, 'Not our public schools. Not here,'" says Taisha Steele, the director of the Virginia Education Association's Department of Human and Civil Rights.[11] Among the strategies for pushing back is organizing parents, teachers, students, and community representatives to speak at school board meetings—a visible demonstration of the lack of support for extreme policies. The coalition has also been surveying a wide array of school district constituents in order to determine their priorities.

The more the community rallies around supporting all students, says Steele, the pettier the board's agenda appears. "One of the big lessons here is that it takes more than one group of people to really fight back. It takes all of us."

Tapping into Rural Resistance

In 2022, members of Reclaim Idaho fanned the state, gathering signatures for a ballot measure that would increase school funding by $300 million a year. The effort put them in contact with more than a hundred thousand voters across the Gem State and ended up providing something of a wakeup call. Idahoans, especially rural residents, expressed real concern about education culture war issues and what was being taught in local public schools. And yet that didn't translate into a loss of support for public education, says Reclaim Idaho founder Luke Mayville. "We heard a lot of people talk about CRT

Reclaim Idaho fanned the state, asking voters to sign a "Say No to Vouchers" petition. *Credit: Luke Mayville*

and their concern about it, and then turn around and sign our initiative that would increase taxes in order to fund public schools."[12]

What they didn't hear voters talking about was school vouchers, says Mayville. Idaho was one of many states where lawmakers, bolstered by lobbyists from national school choice groups and an array of deep-pocketed donors, attempted to enact a private school voucher program in the wake of the pandemic. Unlike many other red states, the effort came up short in Idaho, in part because of deep resistance to school privatization from rural residents. "As soon as they heard a little bit about the issue and the proposal to take funding out of public schools and put it towards private school tuition, they didn't like it. On the face of it, they just thought that was a bad idea," observed Mayville.

The experience convinced Mayville that rural education is the great weakness of the far right's push to expand school vouchers—an organizing opportunity for public education advocates. "It's their Achilles' heel," said Mayville. "They have no answer to the basic questions that arise when you set up these statewide voucher programs that not only don't serve rural communities, but in fact siphon money out of rural communities."

Teachers Can't Do It Alone

In 2018, a teacher-led revolt swept the country by storm. In places like West Virginia, Oklahoma, Kentucky, and Arizona—some of the states where cuts to education spending had cut deepest—teachers walked off the job and took to the streets. Under the hashtag slogan #RedforEd, teachers protested against the disinvestment from public education and the attacks on their profession, often demanding that the wealthy pay higher taxes to fund public education. It was a powerful reminder of solidarity in action.

In the past decade, teachers and their unions have been the leading defenders of public education—part of an intentional turn in the labor movement toward what is often called "bargaining for the common good." Not only have they sought to protect their own wages and working conditions, but also what they perceive to be in the best interests of their students and their students' families. Millions of organized teachers have become a force to be reckoned with.

Yet we can't simply outsource the defense of public education to teachers and their unions. For one thing, unions have long been a boogeyman for those on the right. If public education is to survive the existential threat it currently faces, it can't be perceived as a project of the left. Allowing unions to do the heavy lifting might be easier for all of us; after all, organizing takes a lot of work. But doing so also allows conservative critics to paint the defense of public education as a desperate attempt by teachers to protect their own self-interest.

The second major reason that we can't outsource this effort to unions is that it simply won't work. There may be millions of organized educators willing to stand up for public schools, but they aren't enough to hold back the tide. The American people themselves need to make clear—especially at the ballot box—that public education is an issue they won't budge on. "These problems are not going to be resolved by teachers, unions and politicians. It's going to take regular folks," says Heather DuBois Bourenane.[13]

Perspective: Teachers' Unions Are an Enabling Force for Democratic Education

By Kathleen Knight Abowitz

Teachers' unions are often accused of blocking reforms and protecting bad teachers from receiving discipline or dismissal. These negative portrayals of unions cause many to overlook the ways in which teachers' unions help provide conditions for a strong education in critical thinking.

Why are teachers' unions so important to developing a well-educated democratic citizenry?

The first reason is they ensure teachers a certain level of professional respect, without which, hiring intelligent and well-qualified teachers becomes increasingly difficult. Teacher shortages are reaching crisis levels in many places around the U.S., and legislative moves to silence and discipline teachers who discuss controversial issues are on the rise. Professional respect is protected by union contracts, which help teachers secure fair wages, proper promotion steps, and job security. With better working conditions comes the likelihood that teachers put down roots in a district or school, developing relationships with families and students, and gaining the trust of the community. Experienced, well-qualified teachers are one of the most predictable variables in strong achievement outcomes for students.

Teachers' unions also offer protection from politically motivated attacks by parents or community members. To teach well, teachers must enjoy adequate authority to deliver a challenging and compelling curriculum, which can at times deal with matters that are sensitive or politically controversial. Public school teachers are employees of their districts, and they enjoy limited academic freedom to determine curricular content. Unions can negotiate clearer provisions for academic freedom to protect teachers' pedagogical choices, helping to clarify procedures governing teachers' decision-making authority and the process by which challenges to that authority are decided. School boards can ensure that unions are at the table when developing policies to ensure fair treatment of teachers when their pedagogical choices are challenged. Such procedures can help teachers—particularly those in areas like history or health education—feel more confident in delivering the approved curriculum related to sensitive topics.

Teachers' unions are often portrayed as an enemy of great public schools, when in fact, public education in a democratic society is enabled by them. Unions help create the respect, trust, and security required for good teachers to do their jobs in creating tomorrow's democratic citizens.

Kathleen Knight Abowitz is a professor in the Department of Educational Leadership at Miami University and a past member of the Talawanda Board of Education in Oxford, Ohio.

Relearning Democracy

When Renee Sekel attempts to alert her friends and neighbors in Wake County, North Carolina, to the barrage of threats to public education, she often encounters an obstacle. While people there generally like their public schools and don't want to see them dismantled, they feel powerless to do anything about it. "I hear a lot of complaints that 'all politicians are the same,'" says Sekel, the founder of Save Our Schools North Carolina and an organizer for Red Wine and Blue. "It's a kind of learned helplessness that gives us an excuse not to do anything."[14]

That means that in addition to keeping her network informed about the steady stream of anti–public education bills emanating from the statehouse, Sekel must also make the case for democracy itself. "I'm helping push people back towards the idea that we live in a participatory democracy and that their involvement is a fundamental obligation."

It's a reality that public education advocates across the

country are waking up to. Urging voters to speak out against harmful legislation is already a heavy lift; asking them to believe in a system that's been corrupted by gerrymandering and dark money can feel impossible. And yet in communities that are successfully pushing back—against divisive culture war tactics and school privatization—the result is often not just the defeat of extreme candidates or bad bills. Local democracy itself emerges strengthened.

Despite the horrible threats communities have to beat back, there's a silver lining, argues Sarah Robinson, the education justice campaign manager for Granite State Progress in New Hampshire. "These places are different now. They've had this galvanizing episode that showed them who they are. It spurred community engagement in a new way and the way people are expected to show up."[15] As Robinson and others have learned, the most powerful effect of these grassroots efforts isn't merely them holding back the tide of attacks on public schools; it's watching people take control of their communities.

8

Reclaiming Education as a Public Good

Arizona is in the throes of what the *New York Times* called the "ultimate experiment in school choice."[1] As of 2022, every student in the Grand Canyon State, including those from Arizona's wealthiest families, became eligible for a school voucher. Anywhere from $7,200 to $40,000 in taxpayer funds can now be deposited into a so-called education savings account to be used for private school tuition, homeschooling, or other "education-related" expenses. This includes students who never attended public schools, whose private school tuition is now being paid by the state.

Proponents of the vision hold up Arizona as a triumph: here is "fund students, not systems" translated from ideology to policy. But the experiment underway in Arizona is also about radically redefining K-12 education—from a public good that benefits all of us, to a private good consumed by individuals. As voucher proponents argue, individual families should be able to use taxpayer funds to purchase whatever kind of schooling they want for their children, with minimal oversight.

That philosophy is rapidly translating into budget-busting numbers. By 2023, approximately sixty thousand of Arizona's roughly 1.1 million students were enrolled in the program, which is now on track to cost taxpayers $1 billion per year. In a state that has also dramatically cut taxes in recent years, the program's cost will soon force a painful reckoning over

Save Our Schools members Julie Golding, Signa Oliver, Cathy Sigmon, and Sharon Kirsch. *Credit: Save Our Schools Arizona*

spending priorities. And that is almost certainly the point. For advocates of reducing education spending, the privatization of education becomes more useful the more expensive it gets. As Charles Siler and Dawn Penich-Thacker put it: "As voucher costs explode and state revenues decrease, Arizona has very few options to balance the budget, which leaves slashing programs and services as the only viable tool in a depleted toolbox."[2] Privatization, in other words, begets more privatization.

But what's underway in Arizona isn't merely about replacing a public system with private options. The ultimate goal is to move away from any shared responsibility for other people's children. "The defining issue here is: Do you care about other people's kids or not?" says Beth Lewis, the executive director of Save Our Schools Arizona. As Lewis argues, the fight to save public schools is also a fight to save a vision of society: "Do we want to live in a world that's based on an understanding of a public good, or one where only the individual good matters?" For her, the answer is clear. "I want to live in a society where we care about other people's kids. That's what I'm fighting for."[3]

How Did We Start to Think of Education as a Private Good?

To understand exactly how Americans came to see K-12 education as a private good—something that individuals do for themselves as consumers—we need a quick history lesson. As scholar Johann Neem reminds us, education in the early days of the nation was largely the responsibility of individual families. Those with resources hired tutors or enrolled their children in private academies. In some urban centers, charitable donations to "pauper schools" made education possible for the poor. But for the most part, Americans were on their own.

> *The defining issue here is: Do you care about other people's kids or not? Do we want to live in a world that's based on an understanding of a public good, or one where only the individual good matters?*
>
> —Beth Lewis, Save Our Schools Arizona

As advocates of taxpayer-supported public schools made their case, they initially faced steep opposition. Neem cites the case of Pennsylvania school superintendent Francis Shunk, who in 1838 lamented the difficulty of convincing Americans—particularly those who had already paid to educate their *own* children—that they had "a deep and abiding concern in the education of all the children."[4]

Yet, in the ensuing decades, something like that *did* happen. By the Civil War, Neem argues,

> most white children in northern states attended public schools, and the South was catching up. There was still a long way to go. Black Americans were denied access or attended segregated schools. Irish Catholic immigrants felt unwelcome in schools that reinforced America's Protestant culture. Yet education had become a public good.

What happened? In Neem's view, it wasn't lofty rhetoric from public school promoters like Horace Mann that did the trick. Instead, it was the real-life experience of parents: "In town after town, parents sent their children to new public schools and liked them. More families wanted in. They voted for taxes. Public schools expanded once ordinary citizens became stakeholders."[5]

But even as the public flocked to the new "common schools," the tension between education as a common good and education as a commodity was already becoming apparent. By the late nineteenth century, Americans still didn't receive much formal education beyond what was then called grammar school. Most students left school before the end of eighth grade, and only a tiny minority went on to earn a high school diploma. Those who *did* complete their schooling, however, found that their degrees made a significant difference—signaling to employers that they had the training required for a range of emerging white-collar professions. As a result, Americans began to think of schooling in a new way: as a means of getting ahead.

Universal, taxpayer-supported schooling was initially a civic project. The aim was to ensure the kinds of basic competencies for all young people that had for so long been the exclusive preserve of the middle and upper classes. Scholar David Labaree describes this purpose as the "democratic equality" aim of public education. Yet as Americans began to realize the utility of school for getting ahead—what Labaree calls the "social mobility" aim—it started to transform the way people thought of education's utility. Families soon began demanding greater access to the credentials that mattered, starting with the high school diploma. By the 1930s, roughly 7 million students were enrolled in grades 9–12—a tenfold increase from 1900. For the first time in U.S. history, the high school graduation rate rose above 50 percent.

Within a few decades, the social mobility aim began driving students to acquire even more formal education. As more Americans earned high school diplomas, the relative value of that credential began to decline. In response, students began attending postsecondary education in ever greater numbers. In 1900, just 237,000 students were enrolled in the nation's two- and four-year colleges and universities. By 1940, that figure had ballooned to 1.5 million. And though most enrolled students still didn't earn a degree, the mere fact of having attended college at all became a mark of distinction. By 1950, after the GI Bill expanded access for returning veterans, there were nearly 2.5 million students enrolled in higher education—a figure that continued to double every twenty years through the end of the century.

The aim of democratic equality, of course, never went away. Education continued to deliver a broad benefit at the local, state, and national level. Americans were more informed because of universal public schooling; they were better prepared for the formal and informal rigors of citizenship; and, despite ongoing and systemic inequity, they were more unified. Moreover, public education produced widespread returns to the American economy, which David Labaree defines as a third aim of schooling: "social efficiency."

Still, the social mobility aim continued to exert an ever greater influence on Americans' imaginations. That was due in no small part to messaging from their political leaders, who argued that education was the best way to rise up the economic ladder and the best way to address the problem of poverty. Such rhetoric was a staple from George H.W. Bush's presidential administration through the end of the Obama years. And it had the effect of heaping unrealistic expectations upon the schools, which then fueled disappointment in their inevitable failure to address widening social and economic divisions. It also further advanced the notion that the benefits of public education accrued primarily to individuals who, armed with more and more education, would triumph in an increasingly competitive economy.

Rising Stakes

In Newton, Massachusetts, the signs of education competition are everywhere. Storefronts promise to boost SAT scores, enrich students with specialized math and science skills, or help them craft an essay that will gain them a college admissions edge. An affluent community outside Boston, Newton is known for its excellent schools, and students here go on to college at a rate that far outpaces the state average. As the stakes in the education race have grown higher and higher, though, merely attending a good public school is no longer enough. When admission to a highly selective college hangs in the balance, parents are willing to do—and *pay*—quite a bit to preserve their advantage.

As recently as the 1960s, less than 10 percent of the American population had completed four years of college; for people of color, it would take another decade to reach that figure. Even as late as 1993, when Bill Clinton took office, only 22 percent of adults possessed a four-year college degree. But Clinton and his band of so-called New Democrats began to make the case that college was for everyone. As they framed it, higher education was the key to competing for a job in the modern economy.

Within a decade, nearly 30 percent of Americans had completed four years of college. Ten years later, the figure was up to 32 percent. By 2021, 38 percent of adults had a college diploma, and 14 percent had earned an advanced degree. Though degree attainment among Black and Hispanic Americans still lagged, the figure doubled between 2000 and 2021.

By the time Barack Obama took the oath of office, it was a Democratic Party mantra that education—with a particular emphasis on obtaining a college degree—was the solution for poverty and economic inequality. According to the Obama White House, earning a postsecondary degree was "no longer just a pathway to opportunity for a talented few." Instead, it was now "a prerequisite for the growing jobs of the new economy."[6] *Go to college or you'll be a failure* was the essence of the message.

Yet, expanding enrollments in higher education were beginning to erode the value of the college diploma, just as rising high school completion rates half a century earlier had reduced the relative value of that credential. One consequence was an uptick in applications to graduate schools. Another was that it began to matter more and more *where* you went to college. Moreover, deepening economic inequality heightened anxiety among parents about the cost of falling short. The high-stakes race to get into the *right* college (and perhaps the right graduate school after that) has had cascading effects across the education system and has spawned an entire industry of consultants and companies, all promising an admissions advantage.

Politicians may have convinced themselves that a rising tide of education would lift all boats, but middle-class and affluent families know better. They understand that schooling, defined this way, is what economists call a "positional" good: any individual's gain must come at someone else's expense. The result is a system that increasingly separates winners from losers along lines of academic achievement, to disastrous effect. In his book *The Meritocracy Trap*, Daniel Markovits argues that the battle for elite credentials exacerbates inequality, hampers social mobility, and makes even the so-called winners of the educational arms race miserable. "Today, middle-class children lose out to the rich children at school, and middle-class adults lose out to elite graduates at work," writes Markovits. As he argues, the quest to prove one's "merit" through education is a rigged game. "It blames those who lose a competition for income and status that, even when everyone plays by the rules, only the rich can win."[7]

The political fallout from this high-stakes battle for elite credentials has been profound, helping to fuel the populist revolt that ushered in the Trump era. The Democrats' hemorrhaging of working-class voters over the past four decades was driven in part by the "college for all" messaging that seemed to blame workers themselves for their downward mobility. But this race has also undermined any notion of K-12 education as something we're all in together. When one's own material interests seem to hinge on maintaining a personal advantage, it's hard to think about the public good.

Why Does It Matter If We Treat Education as a Private Good?

What difference does it make if we think about K-12 education as a private good? After all, we expect private citizens to shoulder the cost of higher education even though it, too, generates benefits beyond those accrued by individuals. As historian Jon Zimmerman reminds us, we extol higher education "as the basis of shared national prosperity and progress, then we turn around and present students—and their families—with the bill."[8]

Telling parents to think of themselves as consumers engaged in a zero-sum competition for scarce resources only incentivizes them to cling as tightly as possible to their own advantages. While proponents of universal voucher schemes may seek a hyper-individualized model of schooling—in which parents focus solely on their own children—the reality is that our current system already functions that way. Long before "fund students, not systems" became a rallying cry, parents were moving to affluent suburbs where they could maintain tighter control of their tax dollars. They were fighting to preserve the boundaries of their school districts, imposing strict limits on who could access local schools. And many withdrew from the public schools entirely, preferring elite private schools that could offer even higher levels of distinction.

The consumer mentality has also made us susceptible to increasingly extreme policy ideas. In our previous book,

A Wolf at the Schoolhouse Door, we made the case that school choice advocates envision a future in which schooling is "unbundled"—just as cable packages have been largely replaced by a custom-assembled collection of à la carte shows and streaming apps. As it turns out, we were right: a growing number of state-funded education savings account programs now function in exactly this way, with parents encouraged to purchase their kids' schooling, course by course, product by product, via an Amazon-like marketplace of education vendors. Kelly Smit, the CEO of "micro-school" company Prenda, likens its business to Airbnb for education, with parents searching for customizable content options the way a would-be vacationer might look for a beach cottage.

It's a radical vision in which schools no longer function as community institutions. And yet the reason we are now so vulnerable to such a contorted policy prescription is that we no longer talk about education as something that benefits all of us. Our widespread acceptance of schooling as a consumer good (and parents as customers) can make it difficult to push back against proposals that aim to unmake public education entirely.

Increasingly, the consumer lens with which we view K-12 education also drives debates over the content that schools teach. A raft of state laws regarding curricular "transparency" and parental rights encourages parents to opt their kids out of activities they don't like or subjects they don't support. So far, such laws have been a conservative cause, tapping into anxiety over how schools treat contentious issues like race and gender. But the growing push to incorporate right-wing content into school curricula is likely to trigger a similar movement from the left, further splintering K-12 education along political lines.

RECLAIMING EDUCATION AS A PUBLIC GOOD

Consider, for example, the rising popularity of PragerU. Education officials in Florida, New Hampshire, and Oklahoma have embraced this "edutainment" project that claims to counter "the dominant left-wing ideology in culture, media, and education." As critics have pointed out, PragerU's social studies content is plagued by factual errors and misrepresentations, including a video that depicts abolitionist Frederick Douglass justifying slavery as part of a necessary "compromise." But the real danger of incorporating blatantly ideological content into schools isn't just the risk of indoctrination, it's the further erosion of the "public" character of public schools.

We make decisions about curriculum on the basis of shared interests; public schools are recognized as common ground. Allowing families to pick and choose what kids learn à la carte, according to their political preferences, undermines this vision completely. Don't want a school that offers PragerU civics? Opt out and attend a "liberal" school instead. Don't want your kids learning about civil rights? Shop for a school that teaches the 1776 Curriculum from Hillsdale College, or use state voucher money to purchase a conservative homeschooling curriculum.

The objective isn't merely to change what gets taught; it's to change the way we understand ourselves as a public, such that the very idea of a shared institution seems impossible. And if that's the case, then we might as well stop funding public education with our tax dollars. That's the ultimate end game for the radical ideologues who have been working so diligently to privatize schooling. If we're all just pursuing our own private interests, then why should taxpayers be footing the bill? It's a distinctly nineteenth-century vision of the future—one in which Americans buy their own schooling and the poor settle for whatever scraps they get.

Perspective: Schools Are Where We Make the Future

By Derek Gottlieb

Public education plays a necessary and inevitable role in the formation of community life. This role goes far beyond filling young minds with certain skills and facts. How we make decisions about which skills or facts to teach, how we choose to fund our schools, where we choose to draw district and neighborhood boundaries—all of this reflects and reinforces our most fundamental public values. The *processes* by which we make such decisions do just as much work to realize our values as the decisions themselves.

Public schools are the places where we work out how (if at all) we will live in community, what (if anything) we owe to one another, and what (if anything) we might aspire to become together. We work all this out through every public institution, of course, but schools are the one institution that acts deliberately to shape our future. All of our curricular decisions, all of our scheduling choices, all of our fights over redistricting, and all of our funding battles express our larger political vision about the kind of world we wish to inhabit. Arguments about education, then, are how we think explicitly about the kinds of neighbors we wish for ourselves in the future, the kinds of hospital workers and police officers we would want to encounter, the kinds of shopkeepers and municipal managers we would want to work with.

Public schools are where we remind ourselves that self-government is a social activity. They are where we build the structures and habits to support mutually acceptable forms of living alongside each other. Privatizers target schools because they hope that this can be *unlearned*—that we might settle for a parody of democratic self-government, in which market-based "choices" are our highest aspiration. They want to lower our expectations, narrow our ambitions, and reduce opportunities for collective decision-making. They want to reshape our sense of ourselves as nothing more than isolated "benefit-maximizers" who are related to one another only through voluntary market exchange.

> If we take ourselves to be a democratic, self-governing polity, then the way we do schooling—the things that we teach and the way we choose them, the goals that we set and the way we set them, the resources we commit to this project and the way we allocate them—ought to reflect that. The way we do schooling makes us who we are.
>
> *Derek Gottlieb is an associate professor in the School of Teacher Education at the University of Northern Colorado and the author of* Education Reform and the Concept of Good Teaching.

"By implementing school voucher policies that encourage parents to maximize benefits for their own children, the state signals that the private dividends of education are the only things worth valuing," argues Jen Jennings, a professor of sociology and public affairs at Princeton University. "The civic goods that our democracy requires will not come from the market, but from reclaiming the centrality of publicly provided education for our collective future."[9]

So How Do We Reclaim Education as a Public Good?

We can see that we are engulfed by the idea that schooling is a private good—something that individuals do for themselves—rather than a public good that advances our collective well-being. So what do we do about it?

We can start by reducing the responsibility that education bears for achieving minimal social and economic security. If access to good jobs, housing, health care, and other essentials was fairer, we wouldn't heap such outsized economic expectations on our schools. And ironically, that would enable us to ask *more* from our schools. If we aren't asking them to fix our deepest social and economic inequalities, for example, we can ask them to focus on preparing kids for citizenship in a diverse democracy. Today, we measure the success of our schools mostly according to how well they advance the interests of individual consumers. What college did you get into? What job did you end up with? But imagine if they were judged, instead, by how well they contribute to our collective well-being.

Currently, we ask schools to ameliorate the tremendous damage done by poverty, and we largely embrace the illusion that schooling alone is enough. It isn't. As a result, we not only ask our schools to do the impossible, but we blame them for failing to do it.

Yet when young people have their basic needs met, schooling becomes a much more straightforward enterprise. The best evidence of this can be found in the disparate rates of achievement and attainment that exist across schools—disparities that track very closely with demographic variables like family income. Visit enough schools and it quickly becomes clear that systematic gaps in educational outcomes can't be explained by the innate abilities of students, or by the conscientiousness of their teachers—another myth that is as prevalent as it is problematic. The root issue is inequality.

We haven't always regarded education as the solution to poverty. Consider, for example, the ambitious Economic Bill of Rights proposed by Franklin D. Roosevelt in the 1940s. As historian Jon Shelton documents in his book *The Education Myth*, FDR's vision for a new social contract included the right to a "useful and remunerative job" that paid enough to ensure a decent living. It also included the right to a decent home, the right to adequate medical care, and the right to live free of economic want or worry. Education made the list as part of Roosevelt's broader vision for expanding social democracy, Shelton explains, but not merely because it was a means to an end—a way to secure economic dignity. It made the list because it was an end in itself—something that would help people lead better, richer, fuller lives.

That's a vision of education that we all benefit from. And that's a vision we need to reclaim.

Schooling is what we do to ensure that we live in an educated, humane, and cohesive society—one that is able to reason collaboratively, even across disagreement, and decide collectively. It is how we pass on our shared values and principles, support and sustain culture, and forge a shared ethos.

School never stopped being those things, of course. But the meaning of public education isn't fixed; it changes with us. Sometimes that's a good thing. Today, for instance, most of us would never accept a vision of American schools that was inherently exclusionary and unequal, even though it was those things at its founding roughly two centuries ago. In fact, there is much about the past that we have shed, slowly but willfully, as we have brought our system of education more in line with our ideals.

Yet change isn't always conscious, and it doesn't always reflect the better angels of our nature. The challenge of democracy is that it requires constant renewing. It's less like a feature of the landscape than it is like a muscle—one that can grow in strength, or atrophy from lack of use.

In this moment, then, we need to be clear on what we are striving for.

What is public education? It isn't just free schooling. Instead, it's a system of values that we have created together. Some, like transparency and democratic governance, are as old as the common school movement itself. Others, like inclusion and equal opportunity, evolved over time. Together, they offer a compelling argument for protecting and preserving what we have, while demanding of us a renewed commitment to what might still be.

Schools are not just places where we advance our own agendas. They are places where we come together to become a public.

Rising to the Occasion

In 2022, at a sparsely attended school district meeting in tiny Croydon, New Hampshire, a member of a libertarian group known as the Free State Project proposed slashing the local school budget by more than half. Voters at the meeting narrowly passed the proposal, necessitating savage cuts to Croydon's K-5 school, known to locals as "Little Red." Although the school would continue to exist, it would now be a microschool operated by an Arizona-based for-profit company. Students would learn largely online, supervised by a minimumwage guide instead of certified teachers. For parents whose kids leave Croydon for their education—the town is too small to operate its own middle and high school—the budget vote essentially came with an invoice. They would now have to pay the cost of tuition beyond what the bare-bones budget allowed.

Within days, an organizing effort opposing the new budget was underway. A group called We Stand Up for Croydon Students spread the word about what the cuts would mean for the town and its students. Then organizers discovered a little-known provision in New Hampshire law that could force a new vote on the budget. The catch: more than half of the town's registered voters had to cast ballots in order for the special election to count—so organizers got to work. "Croy-

Over half of the registered voters in Croydon turned out for a meeting to reverse a budget cut that would have required replacing the local K-5 school with an online version run by a private company. *Credit: Jennifer Berkshire*

don has a strong sense of community, and the school is one of the unifying elements that brings people here together," says Amanda Leslie, a founder of the group.[10] And although Croydon is a Republican-leaning area, concern over the loss of its school animated locals across party lines, says Leslie.

When the new vote was held, a record 379 of Croydon's 565 registered voters showed up; 377 of them voted to restore the original budget. "The idea of just taking care of yourself and going it alone runs deep here. But when people really saw what that ideology would mean for Croydon, they rejected it overwhelmingly," says Leslie. "It's a such a testimony for the power of coming together as a community and working towards the common good."

Conclusion: A Fight for the Future

This time it's different.

That's what we tell people when they ask us about the current school wars.

We start by telling them that we've been here before. Because, of course, we have. As long as there have been public schools in the United States, we have been arguing about their purpose, structure, and composition.

Who are the schools for? What ideals should they advance?

What are the subjects of greatest value? Whose customs and traditions should be included?

Who gets to make decisions? Who should cover the cost?

There aren't always clear answers to these questions. And any answer at all is always merely provisional as we wrestle our way into the future.

Yet for the first time in roughly two centuries, it seems plausible that our struggle against ourselves will damage the very foundations of public education. The future we fight our way into, in other words, may be one quite unlike our present or our past.

Prior battles have always presumed the existence of schools that are taxpayer-supported, democratically controlled, and universally accessible. Across the generations, Americans have excluded each other from schools, denied each other equal opportunity, and kept resources out of one another's reach.

We have persecuted each other in the name of our politics, religion, and culture. We have rejected each other's histories. And yet, every September the schools have opened their doors. Our current education war, however, calls into question the very existence of public schools.

Many of the culture warriors crusading against paranoid fixations like critical race theory or Marxist indoctrination are cut from familiar cloth. They are seeking to purge rather than to annihilate. But they stand in solidarity—at least at this moment—with market-oriented ideologues, for whom public schools are anathema. These free market fundamentalists believe that "government schools" and their trappings—democratic governance, regulation, and unionization, among other problematic features—are the product of graft and incompetence. With limitless faith in the free market and a cynical stance toward the very idea of the public good, their ultimate end goal is an entirely privatized system of schooling.

For the moment, the interests of these two groups have converged. Committed market ideologues—of the sort we detailed in our previous book, *A Wolf at the Schoolhouse Door*—are all too happy to advance the culture war agenda. They have deep pockets, an effective policy apparatus, and well-connected political networks. Deploying themselves on the side of culture warriors, they have elevated groups like Moms for Liberty to national prominence.

The groups' long-term interests, however, are not the same. As culture war consumes our attention, market fundamentalists are seizing a moment of upheaval—a window of political opportunity—to drive forward policies that have long lacked the appeal necessary for legislative victories. In the end, culture war isn't merely an outlet for grievance, though it is that. It is also a mechanism for alienating people. In this case, it is a way of prying allegiance away from the public schools that Americans of all stripes have long supported, and which are at the heart of so many of our communities.

The fog of culture war always lifts—slowly at first, and then all of a sudden. Transgender athletes will someday compete without controversy, America's racial history will be taught openly and honestly, and parents will give up the quest to control which books rest on library shelves. At the same time, many families will continue to express discomfort with progressive curricula; many will continue to hold religious values that shape their views of what schools should do; and many will bristle at the tension between individual liberty and the collective good. That's the nature of life in a multicultural democracy. You make peace.

But what will be lost in the meantime?

The flames of culture war have roared through our schools before. Yet never have they threatened to be so destructive. As some activists have mounted the equivalent of a volunteer fire brigade, supporters of voucher programs have rained down a steady stream of fuel. Whether their political moment lasts a year or a decade, they know that the moment will pass. Inasmuch as that is the case, they are acting with all deliberate speed.

This is a moment that demands action. But defenders of public education must take care not to further fan the flames. The response from the political left must not be a quest for total victory over their counterparts on the right. Public education cannot become a partisan issue, supported only by half of Americans. As historian Jon Zimmerman reminds us,

"Activists enter school politics seeking victory and vindication, not dialogue and discussion; across time, they have tried to inscribe their views of evolution, history, sex, and much else. Yet the immutable pluralism of America creates the potential for multiple perspectives and critical thinking in our schools, whether pressure groups want that or not."[1] Nobody can or will "win" the educational culture wars, because as a populace, we are simply too diverse and divided for that.

If we are to preserve our schools, it must be clear that public education is for all of us. We must win the peace.

If we fail at that, we will lose our schools. And if we lose them, they won't come back. That may sound like hyperbole, but it isn't. Imagine, even in nonpartisan times, trying to sell Americans on something as ambitious as public education. It isn't just the price tag, which annually costs us the better part of a trillion dollars. It's also the profoundly inclusive design—public schools are open to all and, over the past several decades, have become increasingly equitable. Moreover, the schools are publicly governed, meaning that they are an ongoing experiment in democracy and self-rule.

Though prospects may seem dire, it is also the case that in defending the ideal of public education, we might awaken the collective will to do more than endure. If we continue to take our schools for granted, as we have for generations, we will fail to recognize that the shape and substance of public education is a matter solely determined by us.

Acknowledgments

We have been working together now for the better part of a decade—something neither of us expected when we first teamed up in the weeks after Donald Trump's inauguration. Even more unexpected, however, is the network of scholars and activists that has helped support our partnership. As the pages of this book and the back catalogue of our podcast illustrate, leading thinkers in education have become friends and allies in our work, and what we do would simply not be possible without them. We are grateful to Kathleen Knight Abowitz, Kabria Baumgartner, Derek Black, Karin Chenoweth, Jonathan Collins, Larry Cuban, Maurice Cunningham, Derek Gottlieb, Jon Hale, Nicholas Hillman, Mark Hlavacik, Ethan Hutt, Jennifer Jennings, Matt Kraft, Adam Laats, Mimi Lyons, David Menefee-Libey, Domingo Morel, Johann Neem, Noliwe Rooks, Jon Zimmerman, and many others. We are also eternally grateful for the friendship and generosity of the late Mike Rose. Our work would also not have been possible without the students, families, and community members who have stood up for a vision of public education that is democratic, humane, and egalitarian. They are more than fellow travelers in this road show; they are the beating heart of a movement. We are particularly appreciative of and inspired by Reclaim Idaho, Citizens for Public Schools, the Education Justice Alliance, Granite State Progress, the Georgia Youth Justice Coalition,

HEAL Together, Pastors for Texas Children, Red Wine and Blue, Save Our Schools Arizona, and the Wisconsin Public Education Network.

Our deepest thanks are reserved for a different set of companions. None of this work would be possible without our families. Thousands of miles apart, each of us grew up in households with an appreciation for knowledge and an orientation toward justice; and, even more importantly, each of us was raised by people who loved us. We are especially appreciative of our partners, Russ and Katie, with whom each of us has made our lives. Their love is the backdrop for everything each of us does.

Notes

Introduction

1. Governor Roy Cooper, "A State of Emergency for Public Education: In Special Address, Governor Cooper Issues Call to Action to Protect Public Schools amid Spate of Extreme Legislation," press release, May 22, 2023.

2. James E. Ford, interview with the authors, June 21, 2023.

3. Emma Brown and Peter Jamison, "The Christian Home-Schooler Who Made 'Parental Rights' a GOP Rallying Cry," *Washington Post*, August 9, 2023.

4. Erik S. Anderson, "Why Billionaires Like Betsy DeVos Push School Vouchers in Pa.," LancasterOnline, September 24, 2023.

1. What's at Stake and Why Should Anyone Care?

1. Alex Ames, interview with the authors, August 8, 2023.

2. Phi Delta Kappa, "The 50th Annual PDK Poll of the Public's Attitudes Toward the Public Schools," 2018, kappanonline.org/wp-content/uploads /2018/08/PDK -Poll-2018.pdf; Phi Delta Kappa, "The 55th Annual PDK Poll of the Public's Attitudes Toward the Public Schools," 2023, pdkpoll .org/2023-pdk-poll-results.

3. Matt Barnum, "The Public Is Souring on American Education, But Parents Still Give Own Child's School High Marks," *Chalkbeat*, September 5, 2023, www.chalkbeat.org/2023/9/5/23859890/parents-polling -surveys-schools-american-education-pandemic.

4. Derek Black, "Old Ideas, Not New Ones, Are the Key to Education— and Democracy," *Phi Delta Kappan*, 2021, kappanonline.org/old-ideas -key-education-democracy-black.

2. Why Are We Always Fighting About Schools?

1. Connaught Coyne Marshner, *Blackboard Tyranny*, Arlington House, 1978.

2. Richard Hofstadter, "The Paranoid Style in American Politics," *Harper's Magazine*, November 1964, harpers.org/archive/1964/11/the -paranoid-style-in-american-politics.

3. Adam Laats, "The Conservative War on Education That Failed," *The Atlantic*, November 23, 2021.

4. Quoted in Thomas D. Fallace, *In the Shadow of Authoritarianism: American Education in the Twentieth Century* (New York: Teachers College Press, 2018), pp. 62, 66.

5. Quoted in Ellen W. Schrecker, *No Ivory Tower: McCarthyism and the Universities* (New York: Oxford University Press, 1986), p. 180.

6. Quoted in Frank Bruni, "Republicans' Fresh Fixation on Vintage Homophobia," *New York Times*, April 7, 2022.

7. *Mozert v. Hawkins County Public Schools*, 765 F.2d 75 (6th Cir. 1985).

8. Albert Alexander, "The Gray Flannel Cover on the American History Textbooks," *Social Education* 24, no. 1 (1960), pp. 11–14.

9. Henry Bach, "Censorship of Library Books and Textbooks in American Schools, 1953–1963," *Journal of Secondary Education* 40, no. 1 (1965), p. 9.

10. Bach, "Censorship of Library Books and Textbooks," p. 5.

11. Bach, "Censorship of Library Books and Textbooks," p. 8.

12. Benjamin Justice and Colin Macleod, *Have a Little Faith: Religion, Democracy, and the American Public School*, University of Chicago Press, 2016, pp. 99–100.

13. Elle Reeve and Samantha Guff, "Activist Moms Spy on Each Other in Culture Wars over Schooling," CNN, May 20, 2023.

14. Julia Grant, *Raising Baby by the Book: The Education of American Mothers*, Yale University Press, 1998, p. 71.

15. Jeffrey Shulman, "The Parent as (Mere) Educational Trustee: Whose Education Is It, Anyway?" *Nebraska Law Review* 89 (2010), p. 292.

16. David Labaree, "What Schools Can't Do: Understanding the Chronic Failure of American School Reform," *Zeitschrift für Pädagogische Historiographie* 16, no. 1 (2010), p. 12.

17. The White House, "President Signs Landmark No Child Left Behind Education Bill," press release, January 8, 2022, georgewbush-whitehouse .archives.gov/news/releases/2002/01/20020108-1.html.

3. Why Are We Fighting About Schools Now?

1. Breccan F. Thies, "Donald Trump Vows to Take on 'Marxist Lunatics and Perverts' in Moms for Liberty Speech," *Washington Examiner*, June 30, 2023.

2. David Weigel and Shelby Talcott, "Mike Pompeo: 'The Most Dangerous Person in the World Is Randi Weingarten,'" *Semafor*, November 21, 2022.

3. Mitch McConnell et al., "Letter to Secretary Cardona," April 29, 2021, www.tillis.senate.gov/services/files/9B070D76-B863-4126-A203 -379AE1B7D22A.

4. Nick Covington, "Current Events Do Not Belong in History Class," Medium, May 15, 2022.

5. Wayne Township Public Schools, "Mission," nd, https://www .wayneschools.com.

6. The 1776 PAC, "Home Page," accessed November 16, 2023, https: //1776projectpac.com.

7. Johann Neem, email correspondence with the authors, July 13, 2023.

8. Greg Toppo, "Irked by Skyrocketing Costs, Fewer Americans See K-12 as Route to Higher Ed," The74, January 17, 2023, /www.the74million .org/article/purpose-of-education-public-views-college-pandemic -future.

9. Quoted in Louis Freedberg, "A Half Century Ago, Race for California Schools Chief Was Most Contentious in the State," *EdSource*, November 6, 2018, edsource.org/2018/a-half-century-ago-race-for-california-schools -chief-most-contentious-in-the-state/604132.

10. Alana Wise, "Trump Announces Patriotic Education Commission," *NPR News*, September 17, 2020, www.npr.org/2020/09/17/914127266 /trump-announces-patriotic-education-commission-a-largely-political -move.

11. Larry Arnn, "Do Our Young People Understand This?" Hillsdale College email newsletter, December 17, 2022.

12. Logan Davis, "The Small Colorado Town at the Center of Far-Right Plans for American Schools," *Colorado Times Recorder*, June 8, 2023.

13. Davis, "The Small Colorado Town."

14. Dill, "Elections Will Never Be a Fair Fight."

15. Steven Porter, "Prohibition Against Urinals Prompts Student Walk-out as N.H. Lawmakers Weigh Segregating Bathrooms by Sex," *Boston Globe*, February 10, 2023.

16. Adam Nagourney and Jeremy W. Peters, "How a Campaign Against Transgender Rights Mobilized Conservatives," *New York Times*, April 16, 2023.

17. Jay P. Greene and Jason Bedrick, "What's Behind the Recent Surge in School-Choice Victories?" *National Review*, February 4, 2023.

18. Adam Laats, "School Board Meetings Used to Be Boring. Why Have They Become War Zones?" *Washington Post*, September 29, 2021.

19. Kevin Roberts, "America's School Choice Moment Can't Be Missed at Midterm Elections," Heritage Foundation, November 4, 2022.

4. What's Religion Got to Do with It?

1. Andrew L. Seidel, *American Crusade: How the Supreme Court Is Weaponizing Religious Freedom*, Union Square and Co., 2022, p. 188.

2. Sarah Mervosh, "Oklahoma Approves First Religious Charter School in the U.S.," *New York Times*, June 5, 2023.

3. Mike W. Ray, "Drummond Reverses AG Opinion on State-Funded Religious Schools," *Southwest Ledger*, February 28, 2023.

4. Robert Barnes, "Supreme Court's Conservatives Critical of Tuition Program Excluding Religious Teaching," *Washington Post*, December 9, 2021.

5. Adam Laats, "The Supreme Court Has Ushered in a New Era of Religion at School," *The Atlantic*, July 15, 2022.

6. Rebecca Klein, "Voucher Schools Championed by Betsy DeVos Can Teach Whatever They Want. Turns Out They Teach Lies," *Huffington Post*, December 7, 2017.

7. Kathleen Wellman, cited in Rebecca Klein, "Voucher Schools Championed by Betsy DeVos Can Teach Whatever They Want. Turns Out They Teach Lies," *Huffington Post*, December 7, 2017.

8. Frances R.A. Paterson, *Democracy and Intolerance: Christian School Curricula, School Choice, and Public Policy*, Phi Delta Kappa Educational Foundation, 2003, p. 107.

9. David Brockman, cited in Klein, "Voucher Schools Championed by Betsy DeVos," December 7, 2017.

10. Brian Lopez, "Public Schools Would Have to Display Ten Commandments Under Bill Passed by Texas Senate," *Texas Tribune*, April 20, 2023. www.texastribune.org/2023/04/20/texas-senate-passes-ten-commandments-bill.

11. U.S. Department of Education, "Guidance on Constitutionally Protected Prayer and Religious Expression in Public Elementary and Secondary Schools," May 15, 2023.

12. Seidel, *American Crusade*, p. 10.

5. What's Really Behind the Push for Parental Rights?

1. Anjene Davis, interview with the authors, July 24, 2023.

2. Patrick Buchanan, announcement of candidacy, March 20, 1995, www.cnn.com/ALLPOLITICS/1996/candidates/republican/withdrawn/buch.announcement.shtml.

3. Milton Friedman, *Capitalism and Freedom,* University of Chicago Press, 1962, 2002, p. 26.

4. Tiffany Justice, cited in Tyler Kingkade, "GOP Presidential Candidates Want the Moms for Liberty Vote in Pennsylvania After Local Victories," NBC, June 28, 2023.

5. Rick Perlstein, "They Want Your Child!" *The Forum*, July 22, 2023.

6. Julie Womack, interview with the authors, June 30, 2023.

7. Maurice Cunningham, email correspondence with the authors, July 31, 2023.

8. Chip Roy, cited in Lexi Lonas and Mychael Schnell, "House Republicans Pass Parents Bill of Rights," *The Hill*, March 24, 2023.

9. Linds Jakows, interview with the authors, June 21, 2023.

6. What's So Bad About Funding Students, Not Systems?

1. Charles Foster Johnson, interview with the authors, June 8, 2023.

2. Marisa Schultz, "Betsy DeVos' Big Idea: Funding Students, Rather than Systems for School Choice," *Fox News*, September 18, 2020, www.foxnews.com/politics/betsy-devos-big-idea-funding-students-not-systems-for-school-choice.

3. "Fund Students. Not Systems. Oklahoma Senate Bill 1647," accessed November 16, 2023, www.everykidcountsok.org/hubfs/Fund%20Students%20Not%20Systems-1.pdf.

4. Joshua Cowen, email correspondence with the authors, June 15, 2023.

5. Betsy DeVos, "A Conversation with Former Secretary of Education Betsy DeVos," City Club of Cleveland, June 15, 2022.

6. Lindsey Burke and Corey DeAngelis, "School-Choice Hypocrisy in Texas Deserves Failing Marks," Heritage Foundation, April 5, 2023.

7. Nicholas Hillman, email correspondence with the authors, June 27, 2023.

8. Joe Kildea, "New Club for Growth School Freedom Polling," *Club for Growth*, August 30, 2021.

9. Jeffrey Spitzer-Resnick, cited in Phoebe Petrovic, "False Choice: Wisconsin Taxpayers Support Schools That Can Discriminate," *Wisconsin Watch*, May 24, 2023.

10. Courtney Tanner, "Utah Voucher Lobbyist Apologizes for Saying She Wanted to 'Destroy Public Education,'" *Salt Lake Tribune*, January 24, 2023.

7. Democracy Is Not a Spectator Sport

1. Alex Ames, interview with the authors, August 8, 2023.

2. David Pepper, "Progressives Are Defeating Conservatives in School Board Elections—Even in Ohio," *Washington Monthly*, August 9, 2023.

3. Kristin Rowe-Finkbeiner, interview with the authors, June 7, 2023.

4. Laura Leigh Abby, "How Do I Tell My Kids Our Family Has a Target on Our Backs?" *The Cut*, July 19, 2022.

5. Karin Chenoweth, correspondence with the authors, August 14, 2023.

6. Allison Troy, correspondence with the authors, August 23, 2023.

7. Zandra Rice Hawkins, interview with the authors, June 21, 2023.

8. Heather DuBois Bourenane, interview with the authors, July 20, 2023.

9. Isabell Moore, interview with the authors, June 21, 2023.

10. Letha Muhammad, interview with the authors, June 21, 2023.

11. Taisha Steele, interview with the authors, September 6, 2023.

12. Luke Mayville, interview with the authors, May 15, 2023.

13. DuBois Bourenane, interview with the authors, July 20, 2023.

14. Renee Sekel, interview with the authors, August 20, 2023.

15. Sarah Robinson, interview with the authors, June 21, 2023.

8. Reclaiming Education as a Public Good

1. Sarah Mervosh, "$7,200 for Every Student: Arizona's Ultimate Experiment in School Choice," *New York Times*, July 24, 2023.

2. Charles Siler and Dawn Penich-Thacker, "Battleground AZ's Bankrupting Universal Voucher Program," unpublished op-ed, shared with the authors, August 9, 2023.

3. Beth Lewis, interview with the authors, June 27, 2023.

4. Johann Neem, "The Founding Fathers Made Our Schools Public. We Should Keep Them That Way," *Washington Post*, August 20, 2017.

5. Johann Neem, "Why Did Americans Establish Public Schools After the American Revolution?" email correspondence with authors, June 26, 2023.

6. The White House, "Higher Education," accessed November 16, 2023, obamawhitehouse.archives.gov/issues/education/higher-education

7. Daniel Markovits, *The Meritocracy Trap: How America's Foundational Myth Feeds Inequality, Dismantles the Middle Class, and Devours the Elite*, Penguin Press, 2019, p. ix.

8. Jonathan Zimmerman, "Higher Ed's Founding Promise," *Washington Monthly*, August 27, 2023.

9. Jennifer Jennings, email correspondence with the authors, September 5, 2023.

10. Amanda Leslie, interview with the authors, August 18, 2023.

Conclusion

1. Jonathan Zimmerman, email correspondence with the authors, August 22, 2023.

Index

About the Authors

Jennifer C. Berkshire is a freelance journalist and a host of the education podcast *Have You Heard*. The co-author (with Jack Schneider) of *A Wolf at the Schoolhouse Door* (The New Press), she lives in Gloucester, Massachusetts.

Jack Schneider is the author of six books, including *A Wolf at the Schoolhouse Door* (co-authored with Jennifer Berkshire and published by The New Press). An award-winning scholar, he is a host of the education podcast *Have You Heard* and lives in Somerville, Massachusetts.

Publishing in the Public Interest

Thank you for reading this book published by The New Press; we hope you enjoyed it. New Press books and authors play a crucial role in sparking conversations about the key political and social issues of our day.

We hope that you will stay in touch with us. Here are a few ways to keep up to date with our books, events, and the issues we cover:

- Sign up at www.thenewpress.com/subscribe to receive updates on New Press authors and issues and to be notified about local events
- www.facebook.com/newpressbooks
- www.twitter.com/thenewpress
- www.instagram.com/thenewpress

Please consider buying New Press books not only for yourself, but also for friends and family and to donate to schools, libraries, community centers, prison libraries, and other organizations involved with the issues our authors write about.

The New Press is a 501(c)(3) nonprofit organization; if you wish to support our work with a tax-deductible gift please visit www.thenewpress.com/donate or use the QR code below.